The Value Perspective

The Route To Civilization

By Jerry Hewes

Cover: Sun Hewes

Edited by: Karen Hewes Suber

Published by Starry Night Publishing.com

Rochester, New York

Copyright 2016 Jerry Hewes

This book remains the copyrighted property of the author, and may not be reproduced, copied and distributed for commercial or noncommercial purposes. Thank you for your support.

Jerry Hewes

Contents

Author's Foreword

One can read and reread this book in any order.

My objective has always been to understand existence. This book presents a new way of thinking, a new methodology for our minds. The methodology changes the way we think by getting rid of material ways of thinking and focusing on how we form our existence: an existence based on the perspective that <u>Value</u> forms the substance of each of us and of all things.

I want to inform you, the reader and doubter of gargantuan fraud; that this book has been written independently. There is no collaboration. I am a member of no organization. I have no title recognized by any modern, materially based, "objective" authority except a driver's license.

I logically and clearly define genuine goodness, as opposed to the faked or imaginary goodness of today's ego-manifesting wealth and fear-driven progress. This book will lead our minds to genuine and rational civility, a product of the Value Perspective.

Sincere Thoughts from My Daughter and Editor:

"If I did say anything at all, it would be this: The book? It's revolutionary. And it's not revolutionary in all the ways we perceive revolutionary thoughts, but in all the subtle ways that can't be anticipated. That quality, in fact, is what spurs the true internal revolution that must happen before any external revolution can. So, Bravo, Pop. You have written your tome!!!!"

Jerry Hewes

Part 1 - Abuse of Our Intellect

Observation

Ask almost any person and they can name a number of things that are wrong with the world today. Genuine goodness is accomplished not by changing the world but by correctly perceiving and understanding existence.

At this time we find ourselves to be the only intellectual creature of existence. We are the evolutionary test of intellectuality and we have viewed existence incorrectly. This misperceiving has created an incomparable mess.

We need to change the way we think to the Value Perspective. Changing the way we think does not change the physical world, but it's safe to say our focus would change creating the "WOW" effect described at the end of this book.

A Glimpse of the Problem

Back in 1955, when I was a sophomore in high school, I helped build a dairy barn with my dad, my brother, and my neighbors. That was also the year Albert Einstein died at age seventy-six, not too far from where I live. I wish I had known the man. My personal life has been most influenced by my Korean-raised wife, and my life-long friend and neighbor Lee Nickerson. On a global scale, along with Ayn Rand, Einstein has been one of the most beyond-the-realm, influential thinkers of human existence because of his extra-professional elucidations.

Einstein sought understanding of existence with uncommon commitment and, as a result, he actually rewrote the book on physics, the most basic understanding of material things known to man. Einstein's search for understanding of existence was resolute, rigorous, and lifelong, but neither he nor those who followed ever found understanding of existence because from a material perspective, understanding of existence cannot be found.

In the early development of Western thought, Sir Isaac Newton (1642–1726) identified and mathematically formulated many "laws" of motion or of physics. They made him the most influential scientist of all time. As far as our existence on earth is concerned, we still use Newton's equations for all common concerns about motion and the lack thereof.

However, Einstein said Newton was wrong, and indeed Einstein has been proven correct. Newton's equations were much simpler and as a result, Newton's calculations are still used today almost across the board. However, Newton was wrong in small, nearly unseeable ways.

Both Newton and Einstein saw the whole of existence as a material happening. But almost four hundred years after Newton, Einstein began to think our supposedly material reality was something quite different than what we commonly think. On close inspection of physical relationships, the material world had inexplicable ways not apparent to Newtonian thought.

By rigorously examining material relationships by non-material "thought experiments," Einstein eventually saw a different reality emerge. It compelled him to formulate his Special Theory of Relativity and finally his General Theory of Relativity. They have stood the test of time, proven in every way by those who were potentially critical of his new conclusions about things.

As the titles of his theories suggest, things are relative and relativity suggests questions about the substance of material things or matter. In Newton's world the path of a falling apple is a straight line. In Einstein's world this path is a curved line whose curvature is relative according to at least five things: its position on the earth, the rotation of the earth, the apple's movement about the sun, the curvature of space, and the curvature induced by things near the line.

While the differences are small, the fact of a difference alone suggests something completely unexpected about a material reality. Relativity rules space and time which also includes the substance of all "material" things, things I suggest are made of Value. Value would explain why the apple falls as it does in response to the inner stuff of its existence or Value and relevant external Values.

Einstein found time to be relative to velocity or the speed of light. Matter and energy became non-relative or interchangeable according to the equation $e = mc^2$ where e is the amount of energy, m is the amount of matter [Value], and c^2 is the speed of light multiplied by the speed of light, or the speed of light squared, a constant and a very large number.

Newton never considered a non-relative relationship between matter and energy, and the equation seriously questions the substance of whatever it is we have named matter, as it differs from energy only by a factor of c^2, a speed "squared." We think of the speed of light as a constant—that is, measurable by a yard/meter stick. Then too, speed includes the factor of time as in miles per **hour** or **MPH**.

All this says our material reality is actually much stranger than what we commonly assume. Matter is seen as inert, but it is really dynamic in ways we will never understand if we think of existence as a material happening. It suggests existence is made of Values interacting in ways we can understand if we realize we are speaking of Values rather than matter. Value always seeks gratification. Science stands upon this **predictability**.

I speak of no difference between matter and life because, with Value as substance of all things, there is no dividing line between matter and life. Everything evolves as the expressions of simple self-gratifying Values compounding to create a new Value having different needs. *Walla*! Evolution!

To invoke the "nature" explanation is a way of willfully saying we will never know how or why matter (Value) and energy can be equal. We blunder on in the subatomic world looking for what is most likely impossible to understand subatomically, the equivalence of matter and energy. We smash "matter" to smithereens in collisions of atomic particles at CERN trying to understand its component parts. It's like smashing a motor apart with another motor to understand from the broken parts what made it yield useful energy.

Matter has no reason to do anything. Then, when matter does do something, it doesn't really do exactly what we think it does. As we move faster, time literally slows down, and we don't age as quickly as on earth. Actual travel distance is always a curved line. At the subatomic level, we find that some information can be instantaneously transmitted across the universe, even though the speed of light (299,792,458 meters per second) is assumed to be a constant and controlling speed.

Einstein is often quoted because he spoke beyond his profession with so much insight. If his words were viewed from the perspective that everything is made of Value (not Einstein's view), one can see that his thoughts suggested a person defined by Value in a world full of people, including himself, who assumed a material existence. That is, he spoke from an unconsidered material perspective to a reality defined by material thinking and was unknowingly stimulated by the Value he actually was. It is why his extra-professional introspections are so meaningful.

That matter does act we attribute to the forces of nature. This assumption of materiality leaves us empty; controlled and defined by nature and having no need of personal desires, rationality, responsibility, or intelligence. So, how do we find the route to mental correspondence with reality? What is intelligence but a self-glorifying name for Value's ability to gratify itself in all circumstances?

Discard the material theory of existence, and assume the Value Perspective, where all things, including yourself, are made of Value. Its principles define what this Value is and how it is expressed. The Value Perspective will in time provide all the answers, leading to an understanding of existence and prove itself the substance of which we are made.

Things Are Not What They Seem

Albert Einstein was and remains today the world's ultimate believer of a material existence. But he examined materialism to its limits and then found himself participating in building something he did not like: quantum mechanics, the manual of subatomic physics.

Lacking the awareness of the Value Perspective, he passed through our world of atoms into subatomic reality and was forced to create a new manner of material thought or quantum (indistinct) mechanics. It was necessary to accommodate what happens when we leave the **predictability** of our atomic existence.

Because Value is seen as an attribute (number) rather than the substance of things, a material myopia infects the subatomic or quantum world, and in this extended search for understanding and meaning he (and we) turned to probabilities to find pieces of probable understanding. But lacking predictability, our material way of thinking falls apart in the world smaller than atoms.

Einstein is commonly quoted suggesting that apathy will destroy the world. But this is only true if apathy is in charge. It is not in charge. The question is, who or what is in charge as our world is in decay and consequently experiences apathy. It is the <u>material theory of existence,</u> a false perspective.

The material perspective is the reason apathy and decay are our inheritance, an existence without any valid moral guidance. This lack of meaningful moral guidance reveals ignorance and results in an apathy natural to the ineffective or faked morals of materialized intellectuality.

If we the people do not sense this flaw and do not know the correct manner of perception, apathy (absence of activism) is the best course possible! The worst possible course is for us to rush off into the never-achievable moralities of freedom, justice, rights, salvation, or collective and heavenly ideals. These imaginary moralities are loaded with contradictions that guarantee killing ourselves to prove ourselves right in a material existence where no right can be found. We are in a situation where apathy is natural, normal, and healthy!

Here, we enter into the intellectual twilight zone where goodness meets evil. Being a material thinker, Einstein was also caught in this dilemma, and he gave it the material thinker's best shot when he suggested evil would triumph when good people do nothing.

Why this conclusion? Because he did not see an existence where everything is made of Value. Instead, he viewed existence as a collection of material entities having no reason to do anything except as directed by an unfathomable nature. For Einstein and us, it has meant our intellectual minds reason with no verifiable foundation and, consequently, have had to create gods that provide some kind of **understanding**. Understanding is our real need.

Einstein's lament about apathy might suggest we turn ourselves into vigilantes who sweep the world clean of evil: this kind of force and commitment coupled with righteous gods compels us to kill for whatever baseless morality we follow. This tacky situation is the perfect breeding grounds for ego or righteousness. The seeds of righteousness are *ideals, justice, rights, all the isms, and gods or deities*. All are unrealistic and all feed egos and governmental ideology with a never ending supply of imaginary rationales.

Most of us are, to some degree, committed to family because families happen through the force of personal Value gratification. But with all of us blundering on in an intellectually imaginary existence, nobody has brought to our attention **what is genuinely important**.

In our morally lost legal or governmental system, activism replaces the potential sense of gratification a family can provide because activism is reactionary and gives rise to and boosts the ego. But activism does nothing to eliminate the next expression of immorality rooted in the ignorance of activism itself. Materially guided activism has no intellectual foundation—that is, no valid morality. Material perceiving is amoral and leads to no understanding of existence except the imaginary.

Nationally, this waste is unrecognized because activism is thought to change the world for the better. History as well as rationality suggests that materially guided activism just kicks the can of ignorance further down the road using the same unsuccessful material ways of trying to make the world into a better place.

Do people who see the world materially see how a material perspective destroys humankind? Have they searched for an alternative to eliminate the contradictions of materialism? It is clear to me materialism consumes our eyes, fighting and far too often winning over any other major thoughts about existence.

Materialism and its methodologies are taken for granted and create our eternal wars of ideals. For this reason, and as Einstein feared, I choose to be apathetic about all modern forms of activism Einstein's thoughts might suggest. Being a rigorous materialist, Einstein could not define what is important and turned to God instead of the Value Perspective and Understanding.

While teaching the understanding of existence is not currently an educational goal nationally or locally, we have the opportunity to teach it to our own families in our own homes. I see my job as teaching and continually exploring the Value Perspective and its applications to our children, grandchildren, and myself.

Some people rationalize that they have confronted evil. We name this "righteousness" or "democracy", but evil just goes on and on only briefly annoyed by the righteous who would attempt to eliminate evil by material methodologies like monetary fines, incarceration, beheadings, and wars. Yes, the material perspective and the belief that collective goodness would arise with democracy is the substance of evil itself. We must finally define evil as it is: "the material perspective," an incorrect perspective.

It is normal and natural that the assumptions of material thought should have enormous problems, as Einstein showed us by moving to the end of materialism where he found the inexplicable (which he named quantum mechanics).

Why have we never stopped to consider that everything is made of Value? It is not a secret. Answer? The ego. Egos cannot be wrong, for they are the outer consequence of an inner faking of existence. The ego is characterized by unsupportable ideals, opinions, and beliefs, forcing minds to turn to dominance to hide their ignorance and find their power by making their pronouncements law. Exposing this body of fakery would destroy the persona exhibiting ego and, for that reason, egos cannot permit this beheading.

We watch evil every day: market manipulation, intimidation, backstabbing, lying, bribing, cheating, falsification, fraud, adulterating, sacrificing for ideals, collusion, omission, overlooking, assassination, execution, marginalization, erasure, kidnapping, beatings, hanging, beheading, poisoning, and most importantly, impregnating our children's minds with the revolting mountain of illusions designed, in the final sense, to make the king of the mountain invincible. Behind it all is ego, endemic and always perverted in a materially visualized universe while the Value we are lies quietly and unacknowledged, trampled by intellectualism called intelligence.

Evil is assuming a material existence. We are currently living a life based on material methodology or the axioms of "Knowledge is power" and "Power makes right," where secrecy, occultism, and money are the keys to overwhelming advantage in the world while a materially enforced morality is in charge.

Note: Although the phrase "Might makes right" is a catchy rhyme, I think "Power makes right" is the best way of capturing this idea. *Power* exudes force and eliminates ambiguity and vagueness.

Einstein was impeccably honest in his examination of a materialized theory of existence, which points to why he never found understanding. His consequential need for quantum or indistinct mechanics frustrated him immensely. When confronted with the probabilities of quantum mechanics, he said, "God does not play dice." His own materially conceived reality forced him and others to define things as *probabilities* or lacking predictability essential to the formation of our existence.

From a material perspective, there is nothing we can do to prevent the world from being destroyed by evil as defined herein because the material perspective is **The Cause**. There is no alternative outcome, no peace, and no heaven. There are only various levels of degradation. Logically following material theory leads directly to "Power makes right" and the growth of a number of evil corollary assumptions to catastrophic excess. It just takes time for its assumptions and technologies to grow and reveal their contradictory nature.

We are well down this path to self-destruction. The egotistical people at the top of this material-thinking mess have no alternative but to follow material dictates to the bitter end lest their egos be exposed as empty and devoid of meaning.

With their backs against the wall, leaders sometimes refer to the "principles" of "this great nation." However, leadership never names them, because they can't. Modern leadership has no genuine understanding of what makes things meaningful and avoids details by silence, evasion, and diversion.

It seems there is no alternative illusion to further divert our minds now that the imaginations of democracy are failing. Materially speaking, the New World Order spoken of by George W. Bush (presidential address to Congress, March 6, 1991) and Henry Kissinger ("Henry Kissinger on the Assembly of a New World Order)," *Wall Street Journal*, April 30, 2015) will become fact.

Kissinger spoke of success as tied to **"... a comprehensive geopolitical strategy,"** a new order of power, a New World Order. This new order does not call for a new methodology but rather the same amoral materialism of "power makes right" and "knowledge is power" strategy applied upon nations as well as individuals.

This material methodology or reasoning has provided all the conflicts of man's existence with the denial of rational thought by assuming a material existence. It is an illogical assumption based solely upon what we think we see and touch, accepted without insight or understanding of what would motivate so called material things to do as they do.

This money based network owes its growing power to the same material ways of thinking, the same time-tested material methodologies employed in the past and today. There is nothing new at all about the New World Order except scale. It now represents the worldwide debauchery of largely hidden and power-groping egos sullied with the inescapable ignorance natural to material ways of thinking. It is still material illusions that rule the day.

Basic Force

In our search for an understanding of material existence, we catalogue every detail of this existence, seeking knowledge, and like Einstein we cannot find understanding. Even though nothing is hidden, existence begs the question why we do not understand existence. This inability to understand forces many of us to believe in gods including Satan, Nirvana, deities, and other illusions to explain the materially inexplicable. The rest of us non-believers are left in limbo, preferring uncertainty to the certain conflicts of ideals and beliefs.

Within this lack of understanding is irresolvable uncertainty about what constitutes morality. Although we may choose to be moral, nothing can be proven to be moral, and all things will, in time, become a reflection of the amoral or materialism's wanton emptiness.

Here and now but largely unknown, worldly amounts of unearned money—that is, money disconnected from the morality inherent in earning it, have become an omnipotent force controlling the ways we think with a number of isms or distractions from the raw material-ism we find unworkable. "Moneypower" does this by inserting into our language and intellects, illusory ways of thinking (ideals, beliefs, and isms) for the purpose of ensuring material moneypower. Included are capitalism, socialism, communism, liberalism, conservativism, and the taken for granted master illusion of materialism.

Materialism is the unrecognized winner of all theoretical isms. With the absence of Value-based morality, there can be only one ultimate material purpose, the accretion of the secret and ultimately occult moneypower. Because this way of thinking is materially inspired, there is no morality associated with it. Its only purpose is accumulating more power and money to establish a certainty of control worldwide. And having no morality, it must become occult to establish another illusory form of meaning and control.

Among the illusory thoughts descending from this insecurity and inserted in our minds are political ideals, the commandments of religious persuasions, and the illusion of economic or financial success. Together these three material vices divert our mind to chasing illusions rather than changing to the Value Perspective. This change would delete the materially impossible task or activism necessary to confront these ideals and beliefs that are essential to material ways of thinking.

The inescapable axiom incorporated behind all material thought is "Power makes right." Essential to its support is "Knowledge is power." Despite what we want to believe, these two thoughts ultimately control the whole evolution of Western thought simply because, in a material existence, nothing can be proven as being moral.

With the lack of bona fide morality or understanding of existence, our minds branch into all manner of material thought, including... supremacy, freedom, enslavement, debauchery, extraterrestrials, heaven, science, knowledge, occultism, rights, righteousness, appeasement, and tyrannical, dictatorial, imperial and constitutional governments, and monarchies.

All current evolutions of these evils rely on force, theories, ideals, beliefs, and illusions. This is modern intellectuality and its presumed civilizations who's essential call must be for equality and yet, competitive domination, an incredible contradiction.

For all of us to think the same and engender peace is preposterous. Yet, the requirements of our lives are the same for everyone.

For this reason we tried to create democracy, to find a foundation in the collective not apparent in personal observation. Despite our best efforts, material methodology or voting for competing views, democracy has turned out to be, again, the power of money makes right. Representation is a myth when practiced from a material perspective where everybody thinks differently.

The existence of religions testifies to the unacceptable nature of the two axioms of materiality, but because religions are still materially based, no religion provides an escape on earth from these axioms. The resulting evil is explained away by Satan and his evil in men's hearts, not by the material perspective, the real cause.

It should be noted that axioms are not principles, and indeed axioms tell us a lot about the way we think. Axioms or commandments and laws are called into service only in imaginary worlds. There are always exceptions to axioms and commandments, as they are essential to imaginary existences and make contradictions impossible to avoid.

Exceptions identify the worlds where governors, presidents, and popes have been given the power of pardons that inadvertently reveal the failures of axioms. This discretionary power is, of course, an open door to all kinds of abuse.

It is exceptions to the rule that enable us to identify imaginary realities. Exceptions deny integrity and open the door to what have become known in financial and legal circles as loopholes, protocols, exceptions to the rule, conscientious objections, privileges, political exemptions, and favoritism.

Axioms are disproven by the existence of love, the exception to the rule of law, which in the genuine sense of mutual enjoyment of life has no need for knowledge, power, commandments, or laws. In other words, all material efforts to regulate love have failed because love persists throughout every adversity, including material plenty, which love interprets as insincere or built upon egos who fake civility, intelligence, status, and so forth. This exception invalidates all of materially faked civility.

As a consequence, love causes separation from the illusions put upon us by egos whose purpose it is to fake their special kind of materialized and politicized intelligence. Love makes the youthful protestations of the nineteen sixties understandable. People turned to love as the antidote for war. War is the fulfillment of "Power makes right" and "Knowledge is power."

Love is the need of the complete body, not the intellectually separate material mind and body. Love cannot be rationalized away. It can be perverted to hate by conditioning; however, hate is essential to separating oneself from what is perceived as harmful and is thus a way of expressing love.

Love exists for the purpose of Value gratification. Incorporated with the Principles of Existence named later as natural to the Value Perspective, love is a function of Value in which our emotions force us toward fulfillment guided by principles. From the material perspective alone, things have no reason for doing anything, and anything done as a matter of material reasoning is insincere and empty of fulfillment.

Love opens the door to the exact function of principles—that is, universal guidance. Principles and the solid emotions they generate provide the best course possible in existence for Value's opportunism, including Value's expressions of love.

Principles are by definition universal. They apply everywhere and all the time. In other words, we should be governed continuously by the master principle of noncontradiction.

From a material perspective, such understanding is impossible. We have no way of genuinely reconciling the wants of one person with the wants of another person, except through the exercise of power as suggested in Charles Darwin's phrase "survival of the fittest."

This is to say that in a universe made of matter, there exists no morality. This is because matter has no reason to do anything. If it did, reason would unify all action to the single and thus noncontradictory purpose of matter.

Civility can never be successfully defined using the material theory of existence. Remember tolerance? It is a must for any material vision of civility. Tolerance is a full admission of continuing prejudice and divisiveness.

This failure to extend reason to rationally and grasp this exposure of intellectual stupidity is not rocket science. It makes one wonder what all of mankind has been doing since the age of reason began.

With all the supposed good will, with all our intelligence and prestigious universities directing all of mankind's thinking, with all the philosophers pricking the conscience of man, nothing has worked as promised. They all accepted a material reality and grew a materially necessary ego incapable of seeing that material reasoning is an amoral dead-end no matter what the philosophy.

In subtle recognition of this, some of the more circumspect thinkers found humility, not intelligence, to be the best reasoning (wisdom) material man has to offer.

The Ultimate Consequence

History has been the collection of unearned money via "Knowledge is power," with enslavement, taxation, and delusional tithing for the purposes of "Power makes right." We have been living in a colossal swamp of faked morality. No genuine morality originates in a materially perceived existence. Matter has no reason for doing anything, and consequently its morality has no meaning.

Thinking materially, no matter what glissando of illusions we follow, our thoughts inescapably evolve to "Knowledge is power" and "Power makes right." This evolution is hidden behind a wall of secrecy (occultism) and illusions defended and supported by the egos of faked and idealistic morality justified in the name of our "right" to privacy.

This secret or occult organization upwelling from this miasma of misperception was in its adolescence called "money changers." They created money that did not exist, in recent history the Illuminati and Bilderberg Group. Now some have named it the Network. I choose to name it "OMNSWO" or Old Methodology New Scale World Order. The controlling axioms of this evolving power have always been "Knowledge is power" and "Power makes right."

We have in many ways already been bamboozled and snookered into the rhetoric of globalism and a single or New World Order. However, we have no legitimate need of globalism, and if we recognize this blunder, their rhetoric will refocus on other materially impossible goals, such as peace, prosperity, absence of hunger, poverty, equality, justice, freedom, and so forth to provoke their ends.

Democracy? As practiced, is also a myth. It has matured as an obvious oligarchy or rule by the wealthy, which means from its infancy to today, democracy's incipient and real methodology has always been of oligarchs—that is, of force and "Power makes right." We thought laws would control this unfortunate reality but even laws are the expressions of material solutions. They seem to be well intentioned but every law, in some degree, removes us from our role in determining our future.

We the people have never been in control. Democracy and all other forms of government must bow before the Network of wealth. The participants in OMNSWO have enormous quantities of unearned money and meddle in very unfortunate ways to control the destinies of nations, cultures, and individuals. Their methodology is to work behind the scenes and through intermediaries to incite whatever action works to ensure their purpose.

We already know the consequences of materiality are unacceptable. Globalism offers no new methodology for humankind. It offers nothing except the opportunity for the Network to skim more profits and force many ways of existing into one controlled system under the still obscure or occult control of global quantities of money.

The Network is the denial of our mental potential and the consequential demeaning of the quality of human existence to our endless struggle against secretive man rather than finding the currently unknown course eliminating ignorance.

With little comprehension of how this system makes the world a sorrowful place, we celebrate Christmas, Easter, funerals, other religious celebrations, national holidays, and entertainment to momentarily escape this egoistic creation of a perverted axiomatic network, which has no principles, no meaning, and no viable vision except servitude and imperialism that OMNSWO asserts is peace.

Their sickness is revealed with the pomp and circumstance of egos faking reverence and civility, about the bad situations they created and we have overcome, to support their insecurities.

OMNSWO's collections of unearned money build to a world scale the same enslavement of our minds and bodies yet to be recognized as the demeaning of our sagacity. That is, in a nonexclusive listing the loss of: acuity, acumen, awareness, brilliance, clear thinking, cleverness, comprehension, cooperation, discrimination, enthusiasm, focus, foresight, genius, good judgment, good health, incisiveness, insight, intelligence, intuition, keenness, perspicacity, profundity, prudence, quickness, thoughtfulness, sapience, sensitivity, sharpness, shrewdness, smartness, sobriety, trust, truth, understanding, vision, and wisdom.

in exchange for:

abuse, acrimony, aggression, anger, antagonism, belligerence,
bitterness, boredom, brutality, callousness, competition,
confrontation, contradiction, cruelty, depression, discontent, disgust,
dishonesty, disrespect, distrust, dreariness, dullness, ennui, evil,
exclusion, hope, hype, ignorance, ill will, insensitivity, insipidness,
languor, lies, loathing, malevolence, malice, melancholy, misery,
monotony, nastiness, omissions, poor health, rage, rancor,
resentment, retaliation, revenge, sadness, senselessness, spite,
submission, subversion, sullenness, superficiality, suppression,
temper, tedium, thoughtlessness, unfriendliness, unkindness,
viciousness, violence, war, wickedness, world weariness, and wrath.

Part 2 - The Problem With Reason

Power, Methodology, Illusion, and Centralized Force

It is natural and unavoidable to have wars in the formative years of "Power makes right." The sponsoring illusion is of peace enforced by conformity. To do this, unearned moneypower or OMNSWO must alter the way we think according to the needs of this illusion. George Carlin said it right when he said, "Fighting for peace is like screwing for virginity."

This power to change the way we think owes its existence not to any moral ground but to materialistic interpretations of existence and moralistic illusionists who can make us believe there is no alternative. Their illusions are ideals and beliefs, plus the accumulation of overpowering amounts of unearned money, amounts so large as to control the individuals, intermediaries, and governments we think direct our futures.

This is evolution according to the dogma of a material existence presented by minds who would be powerless without the possession of enormous quantities of unearned money. Quantities sufficient through political activists and the media, to popularize which illusions saturate our intellects, e.g., global warming, peace and the end of poverty, hunger, or political oppression, inequalities, and global trade agreements. It makes no difference what the feel-good or bad illusion may be. What is really important is the ability of the illusion to increase the cash flow to the sponsoring force.

There has been no change in methodology, and for this reason this "new world order" ideology is just a myth. In place of genuine morality we constantly experience the dictates of ideals and beliefs for which contradictions, conflicts, and wars are guaranteed. It continues with the imagery of illusions we are conned into believing create peace and contentment. They are illusions where war and financial crisis mechanisms serve to increase the wealth and control of the elite as well as demoralize us further.

As the natural evolution of material thought, the occult or secret need is to accumulate more money and power by conspiracy, collusion, and whatever means are required, including marginalization and the termination of all threats to those illusions. OMNSWO has no need of morality, as it is the evolutionary apex of materialism's axioms. OMNSWO knowingly acts without meaning or morality. Consequently, at the top it is secret and conjured, that is, occult.

In all of this, the major material assumption is that "success" can only come from the guidance of a central power. But OMNSWO cannot admit the absence of morality and must remain essentially out of view.

Part of the OMNSWO's workplace is the government we plead to as the determiner of our future. Money, secrecy, the power to manipulate, lack of identifying central location, and cohesiveness only about money, power, and methodology form its body.

The only thing that can expose it is lack of secrecy and people who have enough understanding to read between the lines of any politically correct policy arguments while looking for motive. Being occult or amoral, OMNSWO's participants and intermediaries are tight lipped and vague, only revealing what serves their purpose.

Chaos

Chaos theory suggests chaos is really about understanding complexity in human relationships.

In science, chaos is among other things about turbulence in fluid movement, such as water and wind movement, which can in the general sense be predictable and consequently understandable. Because of their chaotic turbulence, both wind and water have created a living environment that would not exist without chaos's effects. That is, without chaos, wind and water would lose the vitality that creates an inhabitable earth. Any reputable civil engineer or meteorologist can see the turbulence of chaos as both inevitable and essential to our continued existence.

Yet politicians portray social chaos or anarchy as something we must fear. If chaos wasn't perceived as negative, politicians might not have anything to do and we could quit banding together and bending to government.

We are not taught that chaos could be something good in a social order, something our minds were designed to deal with. Such thinking would force leadership to reexamine what is important and get rid of all those who prattle in egoistic ignorance. This ignorance is just what the ego was created for and tries to hide.

Here is a good place to make an important observation. Its veracity is yours to consider. Assuming chaos can be resolved in our favor, the ideals that the minions of civil order offer are simply illusions—that is, diversion and distraction from the hidden (occult) purpose of law. The unsuspected consequence of law has evolved to provide the framework for deceiving and fleecing the public rather than any genuine attempt to understand anything much less how chaos champions our vitality. Chaos does so by providing the environment where the Principles of Existence originating from the Value Perspective can actually create genuine civilization.

It is generally accepted that we plead for release from chaos and anarchy by appeals for powerful and far-reaching state action. However, this fear mongering about anarchy and chaos ultimately results in the application of the protocols of law and "Power makes right" doctrine rather than the teaching of the Principles of Existence in childhood and adolescence.

Our escape from this conclusion is not representation and laws. It is that we act according to the Principles of Existence and use chaos and anarchy to our benefit—that is, we utilize our minds for their intended purpose, overcoming obstacles. Thus chaos is necessary for us to perceive a genuinely meaningful existence where problems exist for our minds to resolve rather than fighting an invincible city hall mired in the protocols and generally inadmissible prejudices of pragmatic law.

It is exceptionally important to recognize the most important unknown of chaos or anarchy is our fellow humans. The sneaky, perverted, illusory, thieving, killing, or evil thoughts of material thinking and the consequences of material theories of existence and how they demoralize behavior and fail to supply the Principles of Existence that would regulate opportunism.

What resolves this issue is that we are talking about universal solutions on these pages, and universality demands we all think similarly. Materially, this is an impossibility, but in an environment governed by the Principles of Existence, essentially identical ways of thinking would not only be normal but demanded by all participants who understand the personal significance of the Value Perspective.

In this Value Perspective existence, we would personally live by our own and universal manner of thinking by *using our minds for their intended purpose*. Moreover, we could trust our neighbor, as competition and its need for revenge goes out the door with the cessation of the material theory of existence.

This would create an existence worthy of possession, an existence that contains an ethereal or unnecessary to communicate sense of communicated trust, a condition we would sustain as the matter of the wholly liberating success of principled opportunistic gratifications and understanding of existence as opposed to laws, guns, enforcement, intimidation, etc.

The chaos we do fear is opportunism without the Principles of Existence. We fear the consequences of "Power makes right" and the forceful abrogation of one's principled or genuinely rational thought process whether by the state, moneypower, or materially opportunistic individuals.

Social chaos has an order we can understand. Today, this order functions unnoticed inside all of us as the intuited Principles of Existence, generally unknown but governing all actions in all environments—that is, complexity in relative relationships.

Our school systems have taught us next to nothing about this reality. This failure is the inescapable consequence of our incorrect material perspective, our blinding ignorance.

The goodness of chaos cannot be understood until the Principles of Existence stand openly in our minds as the essence of non-faked rationality that genuinely does understand existence with this new kind of morality.

Rationality demands understanding. Without understanding, rationales go nowhere meaningful and cannot be counted on to sustain life. The resulting jumbled thinking of modern intellectuality is the result of this irrational situation where we assume the impossible material rationality.

We assume a material reality, even though we struggle to make impossible ideals and beliefs real, the axioms of "Knowledge is power" and "Power makes right" ultimately govern all social achievement. Knowing this, power and faked leadership allow us to go on in ignorance. It serves their purpose and they haven't a clue a problem exists.

Thinking materially, we cannot escape the consequences of these axioms, no matter what protocols, ideals, religious commandments, and beliefs we are led to believe are important.

If we want to know what we work for, we can visualize modern idealisms in a mental thought process, just as Einstein used "thought experiments" to discover relativity. Thinking materially, we can see our existence burst into a phantasmagorical explosion of all things imagined to make human existence better, while we treat our neighbors and family the same as always.

Einstein expressed this following idea. To repeat the same experiment expecting different results is insanity. Just watch science-fiction movies. They're the perfect expression of a material future now that abiotic oil and natural gas or zero point (free) energy might underwrite a materialistic future.

Chaos is a good thing, for it keeps everyone using their mind for its intended purpose. Without chaos, life would be a ho-hum affair with everything preordained and expanding to control by occult determinism, as in the Old Methodologies New Scale World Order or "OMNSWO" we are forewarned about by the likes of George H. W. Bush, Henry Kissinger, and the increasingly controlled leaders in Washington, state capitols, and even local governments.

Governance and Chaos

Despite their claim of inevitability and improvement of the human condition, the New World Order or OMNSWO is just the extension of the same old material methodologies, with the same threats of anarchy, chaos, famine, pestilence, poverty, slavery, tyranny, violence, war, and the like. That is, the "new world order" rationalizes to a world scale the same enslavement of our minds and bodies yet to be recognized as the termination of our sagacity, all because we are told we must fear chaos.

With chaos or complexity in relative relationships, we never know what to expect. Our minds are stimulated daily by the chaotic interruption of the lifeless routines dictated by the material dogma so common to today's suburban, urban, and industrial environments.

If we act according to the presently unknown Principles of Existence, we have nothing to fear from chaos except the individuals or organizations guided by the dogma of a materially conceived existence. They are bent on their vision of progress, progress only enforceable by "Power makes right" and the abrogation of our mental capacities, the dumbing down of humanity to a level that can be controlled by central force, planning, deceiving, and proper funding at the locus of OMNSWO.

This network is the only way to rule in a material existence, the highest level of deception being the selectively secretive Old Methodologies New Scale World Order or OMNSWO, using the same old methodologies, operating at levels of deception above all government regulation. This process is the maturation of the occult—that is, secretive sophistication and the materially inevitable "Power makes right" of which the common man will never be informed.

This inconceivably ignorant, complex, polarizing, behind the scenes organized deception that stirs our pot is the reason we experience so much thoughtless instability today. The so called civilized world is a playground of frictional dissonance, of people caught in the diversionary insanity and deceptions of material dogma and amoral opportunism fostered by huge financial interests operating above governments. They operate behind closed doors beyond all borders in the form of a network of conspiring world class oligarchs, expanding and adapting to a world scale the same material methodologies and techniques that have created today.

Their obsequious self-chosen name "New World Order" is a name chose for its ability to deceive. The New World Order is no different except for the scale of operation and maintenance of secrecy to a level of barely perceptible existence because no one is looking for it. If one looks for the New World Order it is evident in the North American Free Trade Act (NAFTA), Affordable Care Act (Obamacare), the Trans Pacific Partnership (TPP), and the Transatlantic Trade and Investment Partnership (TTIP). It is obvious none of these are public initiatives. Whatever their eloquent content, the real questions are: Who is writing these world changing documents? Who pays for this authorship? And, what is their motive?

Their true purpose is not evident in imaginarily good sounding words because the documents are complex and circumscribe the whole realm with fine print and purpose we will never know about. Regarding the TTIP negotiations still in progress:

Only a handful of people can access the documents known as "consolidated texts", the drafts containing the most recent results of the negotiations. On the European side, authorized readers include the European Commission negotiators, most of them from the Directorate-General for Trade and some European Union members ministers and MPs. Upon the insistence of the US, the documents are not transmitted any more as electronic or even printed documents. They are only made available in a highly secured room in Brussels or in a number of US embassies in Europe. In all these secured rooms phones or other types of scanning device are forbidden. Blank sheets of paper, marked with the reader's names, are provided on which visitors can jot down their comments. On the US side, the procedure is similar, only congressmen and USTR [US Trade Representative] negotiators can access the documents, if they comply with similar conditions. (Source - Wikipedia)

Operating above and beyond governments is no escape from the meddling of governments but rather the extension on a global scale of the same material/illusory ways of thinking. These material/illusory ways of thinking have secret channels of influence reaching into all facets of what turns out to be our distrust, frustration, and unhappiness with most all organizations. We sense we are being scammed.

The proponents grease the hands of those who are most likely to increase the flow of money to central power without regard for morality or understanding. Ideals, including rights, beliefs, authoritative opinion, and secretive organizations, are all represented to be pure and free, just like the FBI, NSA, CIA, and the media. Despite our wanting to see these organizations as pure and free protectors of mankind, they all participate in twisting our thoughts to the amoral and materialistic ends of moneypower our constitutional writers hoped to eliminate.

Despite materially formulated moralities, enough money controls nearly every mind. It is the reason why we invented words such as integrity. Value sensing integrity known as character is the only thing we have standing between us and total subduction. Character is the expression of our overlooked and unintellectualized Principles of Existence. The ego cannot possess integrity, as it is the total function of ego to fake, to throw integrity out the window in the effort to prevent the exposure of ignorance.

If you want to know who populates OMNSWO, look for organizations that were not founded by apparent public demand yet seem legitimate. They include the World Bank and the International Monetary Fund, both founded in 1944 without public or congressional participation. The Trilateral Commission is a nongovernmental special-interest group founded by David Rockefeller in July 1973. The Council on Foreign Relations was established in 1921 by special interests as a "think tank" to direct governmental actions. The Federal Reserve Act, enacted on December 23, 1913, established the Federal Reserve System, a network of private banks that supply money to us at their discretion and interest rates.

The Federal Reserve System is a world-class cartel of special-interest overlords underwriting for a fee our government's money supply without voter understanding. A any organization that operates beyond understanding and behind closed doors has kinship with OMNSWO.

Our Constitution was not the demand of the people. It was formed by oligarchs, the wealthy and powerful, trying to devise a method of controlling the evils so well defined by their class. But, by employing the material methodologies they were committed to failure as some of them predicted.

The Internal Revenue Service was established by the sixteenth amendment to the Constitution in 1909 and ratified, not by public vote but only questionably so by the states, in 1913.

Regarding justification for the formation of the IRS: Keep in mind that our imaginary republic had fought a revolution for independence, and from that time (1776) until 1913 (137 years) had fought something like forty-five more wars prior to the initiation of the income tax. The monetary support for all this violence came from people standing in line for political spoils and the defense industries that would profit immensely from taxpayer support of industrial participation in World War I and future wars.

That's right. As predicted by material theory. The lives sacrificed in these wars were all sacrificed to line the pockets of war activists no matter what their eggheads and the media gin up as moral justification.

To drive this point home is the fact that so called moral purpose is never genuinely accomplished in any war. Both sides are materialistic. It is the material perspective whose consequences yield the world destruction in progress today. While all of us grasp something is wrong. Unknowingly, what is wrong is our perspective. We are experiencing the consequences of seeing the world materially and there is no escape materially speaking.

We must switch to the Value Perspective and its Principles of Existence. The Principles of Existence are our intellects only moral guidance system supported not by egos, faking humility, penance, and sacrifice but by the Value we all are made of.

None of these special-interest actions arose from public demand. They were initiated by groups who could see the potential for increasing the intake of money, interest charges, lucrative and loosely supervised contracts, defaults, spoils, slush funds, research dollars, oversights, and the idealism of political control and economic development. To this our efforts, sons and resources have been squandered.

Governments are not in charge of our culture, even though we believe and many pretend they are. The unearned money of the amoral and material methodologies of OMNSWO and other special-interest industries, such as defense, medicine, insurance and investing always work to affect the way we think for special interest benefit, a direct result of thinking materially.

With few exceptions, governments are simply intermediaries, a diversion from the real game being played behind the obscuring curtain of legal government, the real game of "Power makes right." It has no morality, yet the results must be named progress. This progress has no meaningful meaning, yet we sacrifice our whole lives to whatever it is.

Corruption and Sex

At the personal and private occult level, *all* powerful "Network" organizations use unearned money, sacrifice, and/or perverse sexuality to control behavior because these organizations find their power in the supply of unearned money and perversions of sex.

We need to eliminate this need for hiding of wantonness and actually attain true civilization that directly and shamelessly recognizes the need for sensuous Value gratification. The only way of thinking making this possible is the Value Perspective. In one fell swoop this perspective demands money be balanced with respectful allocation and demands the replacement of illicit inadmissible sexuality with respectful sexuality creating gratifying relationships.

Through sexuality and family it is you, the reader, who will determine the future of man both by what you think and what you omit thinking about.

From a religious (material) perspective, sexuality bares a sense of shame or lack of purity as does all wanting. From the Value Perspective, wanting is the means to Value gratification without which we would cease to exist. There is no shameful sex except sex happening without respect or as a function of material control of men as well as women.

Understanding cannot happen without the Value Perspective. With material interpretations of existence, we have become both resigned and rapacious. Materially, we will always be filling emptiness with illusions. By the choices flowing from sexuality, we make the next evolutionary step to prove the worth of human intellectuality. The choice offered now is the Value Perspective.

From the Value Perspective, **sex is the culmination of all existence**. It is so powerful as to consume our awareness with attainment of sexual congress, and for that reason, it carries with it an unusual power. Ayn Rand writing in "Atlas Shrugged" said it thusly, *"... a man's sexual choice is the result and the sum of his fundamental convictions. Tell me what a man finds sexually attractive and I will tell you his entire philosophy of life. Show me the woman he sleeps with and I will tell you his valuation of himself. No matter what corruption he's taught about the virtue of selflessness, sex is the most profoundly selfish* [Value gratifying] *of* *all acts, an act which he cannot perform for any motive but his own enjoyment—just try to think of performing it in a spirit of selfless charity!—an act which is not possible in self-abasement, only in self-exaltation, only in the confidence of being desired and being worthy of desire."* (aynrandlexicon.com)

And right here, all science goes out the window for there are no numbers and no charts capable of understanding or sensing what is expressed here: the reason why lovers defy bullets. And, if this is true, the culture which follows is also off the charts of science except materially speaking, where wanting, when maligned by every material ideal or chart ever actualized, sums as the ignorant and premature death of man.

The Value Perspective

If you want an explanation of what progress is, watch science fiction movies. *You know, the movies where children play on green grass, among the leaves under trees, listen to their parents, and roam the forests and streams playing and learning about life and finding enjoyable sustenance in the adventure.* Example: Star Wars.

Secretive (occult) material leaders tell us their dogma leads where we want to go. But what we really want is understanding of existence they don't have. With their ignorance comes the application of unearned money or moneypower as the defilement of the human mind.

In frustration with the lack of genuine goodness, some of us wrote a whole constitution with laws and checks and balances of power. That the resulting Constitution did not release us from material ignorance is because it still used the same material methodologies of compelling force. Two hundred years later, we are still told we must avoid chaos and anarchy, or is it really the consequences of material and forceful ways of thinking we must avoid. That once again have in the form of an illusory new government, proven themselves unacceptable.

The evolution of the resulting culture has not led where we want to go simply because our governments have remained ignorant. All representation has done is to reorganize the flow of power. Today, in this intellectual vacuum of materialistic control over creatures made of Value, OMNSWO (Old Methodology-New Scale-World Order) is seizing essential control.

Globalism is another the identifying word because commerce is a source of funding for OMNSWO. With globalism, or financially binding trade agreements, global in scale with numerous legal/political requirements, chaos will have finally been defeated. Along with this defeat we will experience the loss of the sagacity of our minds, minds made to perform in a way that is alive, vibrant, noncontradictory, and self-reinforcing.

41

We need to start thinking rationally, and understand that chaos is natural and healthy, feared simply because the principles governing existence in chaos are unknown. Chaos is the opponent of materialism's and OMNSWO's needed control. Materialism, with all its ideals, beliefs, opinions, and other diversions, has run rampant in our minds, displacing our sense of Value in favor of competitive visions and the momentary elations of king of the mountain, "power makes right" emotions. These emotions always elicit the expanding need of control especially with abundant unearned funding in the bag. Ask the Romans, the Egyptian pharaohs, the Mayans, and so on.

If our unknown principles were known, taught, and followed, we would have nothing to fear because we ourselves would see power as emanating directly from the self in the form of noncontradictory actions or actions controlled by the Principles of Existence. We are supremely capable of dealing with "complexity in relative relationships" and have no need of centralized power. If we assumed an existence where all things are made of Value, our existence would be simple and free of the need for external control.

This existence is described as the Value Perspective. The Value Perspective directs us to the Principles of Existence and Noncontradiction is the master principle of all existence while our intellectualized existence requires five more guides to thought and conduct. The following sub-principles give us the intellectual or thinking, verbal, and active means to avoid contradictions.

1. Honesty
2. Respect
3. Thoughtfulness
4. Cooperation
5. Self-acceptance

With these principles, we can unchain our lives from the fear of chaos. Ideals, while very appealing, are imaginary and contradictory and cannot be reached by material means. Ideals do drive us nuts with their lack of detail, their need for detail, their need for maintenance, problem resolution, and consequential impermanence.

The sacrifice for idealistic ends is not the price of freedom. The sacrifice is the price of continuous ignorance inescapable in a materially perceived existence, the foundation of "necessary evil" or control governments must exhibit.

Material theory must have illusions or ideals and laws to provide minds with some kind of understanding no matter how bad, wrong, and evil that understanding might be. Understanding is our need and the search for it has driven us to all the illusions man has ever known. If the Principles of Existence are known, taught and employed, chaos is normal and healthy, and evil ceases to exist.

Rationality is ineffective in a materially assumed existence because material rationality is a contradiction in terms. It can only be defined arbitrarily, guaranteeing on top of all individual rationalizing, massive defense spending, wars and the opportunity for amoral money to gain world control. Materially speaking, rationality is reason base upon illusion that is used to hype all the arbitrary rationalizations in the name of prosperity, freedom, and justice, the ideals we can never achieve by any material means. Any genuine success by material means is the result of unknowingly applying the principles of existence arising from our substance of Value.

Ideals are powerless except in their capacity to deceive us about the illegitimate rule of power. In real chaos or undistorted life, our natural but presently unacknowledged and untaught Principles of Existence actually become our moral guidance system in the absence of governments. It could be like our imagination of the Old West of the United States of America, where material wantonness is defeated by internally essential goodness, as personified by John Wayne's movie characters and US Marshall Matt Dillon (James Arness) in the TV series *Gunsmoke* (1955–75).

Oddly, two brothers, James Arness of *Gunsmoke* and Peter Graves of TV's *Mission Impossible* (1966–73), define goodness from two different perspectives. The genuine type of goodness is possible for every man, as exemplified by Dillon's character, presence, and problem resolution.

Mission Impossible is exemplified by men of exceptional capacities who slither to and from dictated assignments of mysterious powers. They are exemplified by Peter Graves's character, who follows the politically correct pronouncements of a tape player that must define goodness and then self-destruct for fear of identification by who or what, still a mystery. The former (Matt Dillon) is called living. The latter is called progress. This is the manner in which progressive material thinking affects our minds, coercing our thoughts to the need for control by deception and external forces.

All the materially formulated efforts to control, insure our lack of vision. What we need to see is inside every one of us, but it is excluded from our vision by idealistic illusion—that is, material ways of thinking. Throughout all of this, we seek opportunistic gratification of our Value and desperately need understanding of the Principles of Existence to ensure noncontradiction.

Indeed, the essential question is, will the Value Perspective establish a new intellectual foundation for human existence? Given our inherited materialism, it requires persistence with a great deal of insightful thought. It involves finding the greatest happiness possible with people who think like you do.

There is no truck between the Value Perspective and material ways of thinking. Mark Twain explained, "Never argue with stupid people; they will drag you down to their level and then beat you with experience." This choice between Value-based perception and material-based perception is a conscious decision we will make, whether actively or by omission.

The Biggest Error Imaginable

What methodology do we use to create the culture we want? We have always found ourselves confronted with centralized force and deception. We have never realized we have an option in methodology or how we do what we do. But before we go on, we should realize we are talking about morality on these pages. What we are looking for is a genuinely moral way of life, a morality that is enforced by all of us as the matter of the greatest fulfillment of life possible, not some mind/body demeaning, imaginary morality fraught with sound bites that we accept tongue in cheek, enforced by the priesthood, police intimidation, character assassination, and jail.

No morality arises from a material perspective except the imaginary, the ideal, the impossible, the occult or supernatural, or more simply, egotistically faked morality. From the grudgingly accepted material perspective, we create laws and commandments to shape culture; we force people to conform via the always present "Power makes right" axiom, that strangulating force, the necessary evil.

It makes no difference what or whose morality we pursue. The methodology is the same, a way of forcing us to conform instead of living according to the healthy thoughts arising from an existence perceived as made of Value. It is ignorance, deception, and intimidation (force) that fill all such attempts at morality with failure. Deception and force are the only methodologies we know. We have no understanding of existence, no verifiable morality.

Genuine rationality must contain genuine morality. In order for reason to be truly rational it must incorporate a morality that always supports our life. This morality must be personally ours alone and it must be rationally reasoned to sustain our Value with the Principles of Existence.

Intellectually, all this means we are in the medieval "Age of Reason" where reason and tolerance for many differing moralities are thought to create rationality and civilizations. But if existence is conceived materially, no genuine foundation exists for any morality because matter provides no reason for doing anything.

To this day, all official reasoning and believed rationality is based entirely on whim or a vision of God, Nirvana, deities, etc. It's even on our money!

Common sense is our way of saying reason should be supported by our intuited Value while we view and argue things materially. Here, we have lost the battle for personal control of our existence to moneypower and its totally material view. By using the material perspective, we are all prevented from seeing the universal morality, the common sense the Value Perspective supplies—that is, the Principles of Existence.

To escape lack of meaning we should be using the Principles of Existence incorporated with reason—that is, rationality! Until we unite in universal morality, with a genuine intellectual foundation, we are still living in the "Age of Reason," or intellectually, the 17th (1600s) century.

We try to think the "Age of Reason" was followed by the "Age of Enlightenment," or scientific revelations and existentialism, and the New World Order. But all have been obfuscations of truth with complete intellectual bondage to materialism simply because the material perspective prevented us from seeing the light.

All rationality, if it is to be rational, must include universal morality—that is, the Principles of Existence. These principles find their origin in the incontrovertible assumption that we and all things are made of Value.

Rationality must support life or it is not rational. And essential to survival, rationality must make existence worth possessing. There must be gratification of Values or everything ceases to exist. Only the Value Perspective yields the Principles of Existence morality we need to insert into reason because Value is the only thing to be preserved. If there is no Value, there is no reason for anything!

Noncontradiction of Value is the foundation of all genuinely good intellectuality, something everyone should know by early adolescence if not before.

Making this assessment is impossible from a material perspective because material interpretations of existence cannot even visualize things made of Value.

Thinking materially, we can gin up any reason we want, and indeed we do, from the occult, to cereal box fairylands, to genocide, and racial purity, to gods, heaven, hell with alien and reptilian intervention, all in response to the emptiness of materially based reason.

Modern material progress—that is, money and the class-isms it offers, psychologically underlies urban blight, shootings, chemical dependency, crime in general, sexual trafficking, nearly all mental illness, pollution-induced illness, malnutrition, dysfunctional families, and economic insolvency at the hands of professionals such as educators, doctors, attorneys, judges, politicians, and the like. They all pretend to help while they all place us on the outside of things kept secret or occult because they operate from a foundation of ignorance that cannot be admitted as ineffective, the ego.

This professionalism is the other side of the same coin with the depravity it confronts. It is the license to stand beyond commonality and execute illusion and control over our ignorance. Imagine how things would change if professionals were replaced by those who are wise instead of broadcasting the protocols of material reasoning and exhibiting the failure to know what is important.

If we look at how such people are chosen, we can see the degree hanging on their wall whose ultimate authority stems from a government materially constructed for some imaginary end. We have yet to recognized the ends of this system of progress cannot be reached by material methodologies. There is no end evident in materially based thought consistent with happiness and contentment. For the professional, the poor and impoverished classes define the lack of professional success rather than honoring the proving ground of humanity from which all of us arise.

There is no Value in this system. Its reasoning goes nowhere meaningful except to power and force unless it is guided by rationality, and rationality is not rational unless it genuinely knows that we are made of Value—that is, physically palpable Value.

Value does not become an "ism" like materialism, communism, or capitalism because it is not an imaginary ideal like all the other isms. It is an eternal, enduring, and unchanging fact of existence and we unknowingly give it that honor in our language by never having the need to make Value an ism.

Every material manner of thought falls into various categories of limbo, where people are forced to admit they don't know in the ultimate sense. They frequently feel compelled to reference God. It brings the issue of knowledge into sharp focus as we seek knowledge under the premise that it will answer all questions but it never has, not even close.

The question becomes, for what purpose does knowledge exist? Answer: Knowledge is power, the imaginary power to preclude chaos. Its role in our thought patterns confirms that knowledge's function is to increase power in a meaningless and amoral environment making peace an impossibility.

We can jump behind the scene here. Truth has surfaced in print, screaming for the materialist to name the knowledge that is the exception to this condemnation.

We want to say material knowledge is certain and restore the "civilization" that was nascent in the good old days of exploration. We want to label the Value manner of thinking as poppycock. But we can't. We are confused about what is important. Materially speaking, naming what is important is impossible.

There is no more fundamental thinking anywhere in the universe than what is being discussed with these words. We stand here and now at the evolutionary origin of all apparent rationality and are witness to the destruction of the quality of human existence.

At this moment we stand at the depth of this destruction, with imaginary democracy, representation, and professionalism creating a multitude of destructive consequences only materialistic reason coupled with egos can manufacture. Our only saving grace is something characterized by "common sense."

Genuine rationality can only surface in today's intellectual climate by denying much current sophistication. Our materially faked civilization fills our minds with great-sounding schemes called ideals, rights, justice, equality, progress, and the ever more irrational globalism. All are supported by invincible egos worshiping amoral money—that is, money whose morality is that of materially misdirected and ignorant reasoning.

Jerry Hewes

Part 3 - Is there A Solution?

Jerry Hewes

The Path

Could it be we want understanding?

Ever walk through the woods and find a path
on a most enjoyable day when the leaves
are ripe with gold as they fall at your feet
where wild animals have passed many times?

This path is meaningful
with no end and no beginning.
Animals enter and depart
freely as their Value dictates.

For them the path itself
makes life an enjoyable experience,
providing direction and security
all the security the world has to offer.

This path is not for us
on our way to freedom, liberty, and justice
multitudes with no common route
except to chase an end.

The lack of freedom is
a necessary evil, we are told,
to escape the ravages of chaos created
when everyone takes freedom seriously.

Appreciation and reverence never were;
freedom, liberty, and justice haven't arrived.
On through the ages this rumbles,
with sacrifices since time began.
We treat our neighbors no better.

The Value Perspective

The marvels of intelligence will save us.
Game loaded with many systems,
each certain for freedom, liberty, and justice,
but they never arrive.

A world so dependent upon energy
questions the very existence of man;
a world consumed with security
builds the bombs of mutually assured destruction.

Intelligence says we are in control;
progress is our mandate.
So smile and the risk disappears,
but wisdom says it will happen.
Intelligence will compound the fall.

Intelligence defines all.
No paths, only vague terminals
for freedom, liberty, and justice.
This is the storyline told.

Down this route we go.
There is nothing else to note.
Boredom our lot,
entertainment our distraction,
progress our destruction
the path of barren minds.
Freedom, liberty, and justice never happen.
What form would they take if they did?

We cry as we shake our wooden legs;
our glass eye rolls into the sink.
It seems we are up a tree
sitting there for a moment's pass
to watch the animals go by.

We discover quite another path
going hither and thither to no end at all,
yet it serves its purpose well.
Many appreciate its substance.
Many follow its reality.

What is the substance of reality
so bleak as to escape attention?
For some inexplicable reason
our minds set to behold
a world of mud, thunder, and death,
our minds so dead to seeing.

It is to another realm we look
to freedom, liberty, and justice,
the matter of ideals,
full of paths only apparent,
never reaching the vague ends.

From above we look
at the ground, at the path
we were ordained to follow
but could find no reason why.

Though myths abound of sacrifice and glory,
they're not reality
they ask nothing of inside,
yet they steal our hearts away,
frittered to the harlots
of reaction, revenge, illusions.
Consumed by ignorant minds,
they've never saved the day.

On we go to progress
while our minds begin to sway,
until the fateful moment when
our caring is filled with hate.
We are so looking outward,
the music of the state.

In all the hurt and sorrow
the rowdy crooks play.
They're the mentors of our sorrow
freedom, liberty, and justice
the illusions of their way.

"This cannot be," our minds complain.
Meaning never comes,
so where to turn?
We grasp an empty bay.

Where we have not been
we cannot know the fruit.
We leave it to the doctors, but
they have not looked either,

Objectivists lament,
subjectivists feel,
materialists mechanicate,
spiritualists magnificate.
Rationality escapes our grasp.
There is no foundation.

We have sung our song
and come up empty still;
emptiness forces us to ask.
The crow and deer never ask
but find existence anyway
of sustaining meaning,
of importance understood.

Are we not also participants in existence?
What chance of thought excludes us
from understanding existence?
Failing to look within for guidance?
The crow and the deer always do.

Jerry Hewes

What is important?
Ask any sage;
you will find no mystic
ringing the bell of meaning or understanding.

Material things have no reason to do anything.
Read it however you like.
No rationality possible;
no meaning or understanding forthcoming.

So spirit and soul
become our lot,
this vision of matter
where matter matters not,
of worlds divided and wars fought
along those paths of slippery glory.

We are as intellects go
of beliefs and ideals impossible,
of toothless rationales
pretending to be real.

I spoke to my wife
about this charade,
the Scrooges of Values sought
and sold for trade
while the zeros fly by
in useless parade.

Talking to her flowers
it is Value that speaks.
Without Value there is naught
sailors upon the water with
no ship, no compass, no land.

The Value Perspective

Full speed ahead in blinding, colorless light.
None see or smell the flowers.
The leaders ply their trade but
know not where they lead.
They counterfeit our day.

Flowers' Value reaches out
to stimulate minds
of what we are about.
Their Value is expressed.
Do we think we are different,
or is it true
we too are made of Value?

What would it be that anything does
were it not for the Value it is?
Rather than possession
Value's function is to express,
to seek gratification.
The meaning lasts forever
of magnificence unconnected to ignorance.

Matter has no reason,
strange we should think it does.
We defer reason to nature,
leaving our minds to wander on,
and nature answers not
for understanding sought.

Though we too are nature sublime,
no animal but man
willfully abandons his mind
matter the locale of nothing,
nature the sorry excuse of ignorance.

To look within
is to wipe nature away
and recognize
Value gratification is all.

The materialist complains
civility is gone,
chaos the result
of freedom sought
but never found,
dead as the consequence
of self-inflicted contradictory wounds.

Long live the king,
but he is gone.
The fawning has failed
the violence upon our minds,
the sacrifice of self.

Then flowers bloom
o'er the grave,
expressions of Value
for flowers' day.

Why do flowers bloom
and not succumb?
Nothing imagined, even unreal,
could permit contradiction
of Value's expressions.
It is so sacred, so real.
Existence itself
depends on contradiction's absence.

We have minds to this date defeated,
lost in a world of ideals,
of words contorted and twisted,
of promises aborted
while civility waits at the door.

What manner of progress
do we need?
It seems progress is the weed.
It is to be honest,
to accept as our creed
the need of clear inner honesty.

It is only with this honesty,
the will to respect all men,
that we show the wisdom
of life without contradiction.

Oh my goodness,
what can it be?
The life of goodness,
simple as one, two, three.

Noncontradiction, honesty, and respect—
the pillars defining truth and goodness.
We have not sought;
we think materially.

The story of Value expressed goes on
with thoughtfulness the manner supreme,
making all the foregoing possible
the foundation of life with understanding.

In the Declaration of Independence
"the pursuit of Happiness"
it seems is never
mentioned again.

The happiest of days are spent
in cooperation
where fear does not exist.

Happiness is a common cause
leaders have not found.
Bedeviled by material ideals
steeped from beliefs about reality
nurtured by disparities,
lost to ideals of no meaningful substance,
their blinded eyes only see
the men who grab materially
the Values of the day.

They never stop to think
life's simply a path,
any end sought
unreachable,
benefits not any moment.

Leadership has no gravity,
only beliefs, assumptions, illusions.
Depraved is just one variant
seen only from one perspective.

The state, the only remedy,
has so many knowings
but understands not.
The methodology is force,
its source our sacrifice

of minds commanded to follow leadership,
ignoring those wanting to understand
what goodness is and how it is found.
We come face-to-face with opportunism,
whose guileful tricks of no meaning
only lead to material pots.

The charade is played;
the game wanders on.
Materialist claims of reality
drip caustically on the wasting earth.

The Value Perspective

We have not added two to two;
we are more ignorant than in childhood.
Indeed, how can two be added to two
when contradictions are permitted?

What say we now?
We have smitten our integrity.
Substance was never here.
We wait for the bomb,
having no meaningful course correction
because ego thinks we're all.

Life is of the moment.
While going down the path,
this route is meaningful,
with no end and
only choice for a beginning
of life and enjoyment,
providing direction and security,
all the security the world has to offer.

While walking down the path,
we discover the life-sustaining guidance:
noncontradiction … honesty … respect …
thoughtfulness … cooperation … self-acceptance last,
for self-acceptance is not our choice
until the principles are
complete with our understanding
of goodness. The principles make
a path with no contradictions,
every reason to integrate, to enter.

Jerry Hewes

This is integrity
the world cannot find today,
the path of contentment in everything we do
because we understand
Value is existence,
ours to appreciate.

J. Hewes

Observations 2

Principles define Value and make existence genuine.

Value, and the principles defining it, make understanding possible.

Knowledge changes from day to day, and what is true one day may not be true the next day or in the next millennium.

The pursuit of knowledge forces us to the impossibility of knowing everything which is a total diversion from understanding, happiness, and contentment.

Understanding only requires we know the operating principles by which everything acts.

Understanding of existence is directly connected to happiness and contentment.

The Value Perspective and its defining principles always answer the question why.

To assume everything including us is made of Value changes nothing, except the way we think.

The way we think is **The Problem!**

Opening the Door

Henry David Thoreau wrote, "I went to the woods because I wished to live deliberately, to front only the essential facts of life, and see if I could not learn what it had to teach, and not, when I came to die, discover that I had not lived."

When I was 49, I went to the woods a zero, alive but having no understanding. In two weeks of searching, I finally asked, "What is important?" Materially speaking, I had asked the impossible question but the Value I am soon responded with "I am Value."

My Value had weeded out the impossible nature of the question and responded with a puzzling "I am Value." It did not seem to directly answer the question because the syntax seemed somewhat twisted. Yet immediately my body was filled with a sense of meaning. Why? Because my immediate and continuing purpose then became gratifying this Value. To be sure, there were many unanswered questions. Some of them were answered quickly.

- If I am made of Value, then ***noncontradiction*** of that Value is paramount. This is the foundational or master principle of all existence.

- For noncontradiction to be an effective principle, one has to be absolutely ***honest***. This level of honesty goes beyond traditional honesty with other people to honesty about every internal thought.

- An unsettling conversation with my brother forced me to examine what unsettled me. The resolution resided in recognition of the absence of ***respect***. Respect tells us how to successfully interact in all relationships.

- What makes all of this happen? ***Thoughtfulness***. It's why we have a mind. But there seemed to be much more to examine, and it took some time to figure it out.

- It seems that our happiest moments are working noncontradictorily with self, family, and others. We call this ***cooperation***. Cooperation is the source of all happiness, be it with the self, a spouse, a mother-in-law, a child, neighbors, even enemies. Still something is missing, because this alone does not make us contented with what we are.

- The unobvious answer is ***self-acceptance***. It is unobvious because self-acceptance only becomes real, possible, and perceived when one has incorporated all the previous principles into his way of thinking.

We do not even know contentment (self-acceptance) is possible until we employ the five previous Principles of Existence. Contentment says, "I know what is important, and it does not require more wealth or power." Contentment requires that I live by these Principles of Existence so I can know I have lived honestly and genuinely—that is, a heart and mind at peace with their actions and the ability to think successfully.

These are the guiding Principles of Existence or morality of the Value Perspective.

Reason

Reason is used to manage everything from imaginary to concrete facts of existence. Reason originates with how we think existence is organized. If we perceive existence incorrectly, our reasoning will generate false conclusions that negatively affect our ability to make existence an event worth possessing.

The consequences tell us that, far too much, we perceive existence incorrectly. Within the scope of reason is an unlimited mine field of mistaken and consequently destructive beliefs. They are unfortunately considered to be a normal part of proper human existence but, they are not a normal part of human existence. They are only normal to a reason-based existence that is unable to define materialism rationally. This consequence forces us to turn to ideals and beliefs. Our task is to understand two different ways of thinking.

I.   The material way of thinking and reasoning. This is an overwhelmingly popular, powerful, and incorrect perspective. (If reasoning always produced correct results, the word rational would never have been created.)

Used alone material reason will lead to the complete destruction of life, as when material plenty brings into question the earth's ability to sustain our wastefulness or when the military becomes capable of creating an uninhabitable world nearly instantaneously, or some other excess created by reason.

II.   The Value Perspective is genuinely rational—that is, productive of what we genuinely need. The Value Perspective is constantly active, but generally unacknowledged because it is constantly taken for granted and powerless in most any modern legal, social, and intellectual relationship. But Value is always present hopefully moderating most discussions towards what is rational when they become absurd in their material conclusions.

Religion and Belief

Seeing is believing, according to the old adage, but what we see may be interpreted inappropriately, especially if we assume an incorrect perspective. An incorrect perspective seems unlikely, as we live in a material universe, don't we? Or would it be more appropriate to say we are living a *theory* of existence called materialism? Are not all political theories of existence called isms?

That we routinely assume a material existence does not make the material perspective anything less than a mistake. It would explain why we are so obsessed with making the world a better place by forcing people to be "good" and getting all kinds of adverse and reactionary consequences.

Unknown to politically correct politics, to modern objective thought, to economic leadership, to materially guided education, to directionless, easily manipulated science, and to any modern leadership or egos is, "The Value Perspective." It's not a theory. We have by agreement chosen not to make "valuism" a word.

The first step to ending the madness and insanity of reasoned material thinking is to accept the premise that we and all things are made of Value. This is what is important: ***more important than anything else in human existence***. Failure to realize this fact will prematurely terminate this so-called intelligent species of life because we are unable to determine what is important.

If one examines the Value Perspective in depth and breadth, it becomes apparent that the Value Perspective is complete! We can understand everything. Theories do not have this completeness. Material theory is full of inexplicable problems created not by nature but by our inability to reason materially to rational conclusions.

Several rationales explain why we may not live in a material universe, and the biggest one is the rationale of God. What is He made of? An offensive question? Maybe, but we have minds capable of most any expression, and to ignore this material one is, I think, irresponsible, especially if we pretend to rationality. If we perceive reality correctly, why is there a need to believe? None of material reality is hidden from us, and yet we persist in believing.

Religion is one of many material ways of thinking to explain away lack of understanding. But one word cuts to the heart of the matter, why? The subject of this unanswerable question comes to us clearly on our dollar—In God we trust—. We have no understanding of why. This emptiness forces us to believe in God as an indisputable and irrefutable vision that explains away the vagueness of a material existence and the seemingly meaningful question of His substance is ignored because it is materially and meaningfully unanswerable.

The existence of belief says that material perception is at best incomplete. Thus our whole existence here on earth is premised upon a wantedly complete but at best incomplete material imagination. Here, it is clear we seek understanding unavailable from material perceiving which also points to the incorrect nature of viewing existence materiality. At the deepest levels of inquiry, materiality's standard response is always, "I don't know." to minds seeking understanding.

Seeking understanding, many of us have turned to beliefs in hopeful rejection of material consequences. Thinking materially, we must believe and have theories of existence. But ideals, beliefs and laws are no substitute for failing to use the Principles of Existence arising from the Value Perspective.

They are only the wishful expressions for a material existence from which there is no understanding, no escape. When believing fails, the so-called objective thinkers and scientists go back to the drawing board and create new or adjusted theory of materialism that is still bound by beliefs, ideologies, laws and other material ways of thinking.

They think materially guided reason will prevail. Contradictions inherent in ideals and beliefs do not permit material reasoning to prevail. These contradictions foster only continuous turmoil and intermittent war, intermittent only because of periodic exhaustion.

Consider our ultimate scientific direction to date. The field of quantum physics is charged with understanding the smallest known material particles of existence, based on the premise that understanding originates there. It does not. But empire building or continued material scientific funding guarantees a massive distortion of direction towards ways of debasing and destroying our Value.

Einstein forced quantum mechanics into existence by rigorously visualizing a material theory of existence. He was rewarded with probabilities and, as a result of lacking predictability, ***neither knowledge nor science***, a fact overlooked by modern intellects.

Einstein, our supreme materialist, refused to accept the illogical material assumptions of quantum mechanics with the extraprofessional statement, "God does not play dice." As a result the major direction of quantum mechanics funding is for the yet to be revealed dark and occult art of human destruction, the defense industries, the violation of everything predictable and good as a function of the games of probabilities.

Quantum mechanics is, at its root, the search for meaning we have not found in a predictable materially viewed atomic existence. In the subatomic or quantum realm, predictability lapses, and without predictability, building a conventional materially theorized understanding is impossible. In other words, quantum or sub-atomic mechanics is the study of deconstructed, unconstructed, or non-existent existence, and we are doing no better at understanding this subatomic realm under material assumptions of existence than we have in our predictable atomic or elementally based existence.

As a consequence we have become egos following the imagined necessity of protecting faked civility no matter what error in probabilities will certainly happen at some point down the road.

This outside the self-search for knowledge has led us socially down a dead end street of science having no understanding of goodness. All of this happening because we search materially for understanding which cannot be found materially. Understanding can only be found in our minds and it means our minds are a complete "thing" of Value, where every action is designed to gratify this Value and it cannot be done without understanding. Yet, understanding is impossible to achieve materially speaking. Science has become reason exclusive of rationality.

We are, today, verifying the ultimate consequence of thinking materially. The resulting thought patterns have brought us to an existence so corrupt that we face the destruction of our living environment. The rise of amoral unearned money to indisputable power, always intervenes in the course of social organization, industry, civil unrest, media, science, and law to keep the human body in slavery to money.

It happens because we lack understanding, not the ideals of freedom, justice, rights, nor heaven. No one has ever related how these imaginations actually work together or reinforce each other to give humankind happiness and contentment. All of these illusions are just reactions to the complete failure of governments, our ideologies, and beliefs.

In facing a material reality, we must ask, what proof do we have that the material perspective is the correct perspective? If a material perspective leads us to correct results, why need we spend all our money trying to fix what is thought to be good and meaningful? If the material perspective is wrong, we have no escape except the supernatural or beneficent alien rescue some people already know contains evil or... changing to the correct Value Perspective.

Every ill of our culture owes its origin to material ways of thinking—that is, to the force necessary to rearrange or reform "matter" including us, to some ideal of perfection, rather than changing the way we think. Changing not to some other ism, but to the employment of the Principles of Existence where the mind itself creates genuine gratification through how it thinks about relationships.

Progress in Understanding

Noncontradiction is where our salvation lies.

Understanding can only occur in a realm having no contradictions. Contradictions prevent understanding by contradicting each other. This is a very simple, irrefutable observation. There is no way to understand irreconcilable ideas.

We have yet to acknowledge that we always seek understanding of existence. Those who do not seek understanding are those who enforce political correctness, the illusionists, the fakers of civilization, the egos.

The pursuit of knowledge in a materially envisioned existence does not lead to understanding of existence. It leads to occultism. Knowledge evolves to the full application of the two axioms of materiality, "Knowledge is power" and "Power makes right" with the consequential need for secret, mysterious, and extreme control having no admissible argument for understanding or goodness except incomprehensible powers, i.e., the occult.

Materiality offers no noncontradictory understanding of our opportunism and must muddy the waters with ideals, beliefs, and rights, or synthetic morality because the consequences of materialistic (amoral) opportunism are unacceptable to common sense man.

The Value Perspective accepts opportunism as healthy, the only way in which life prospers with the application of noncontradiction and the five consequential principles of honesty, respect, thoughtfulness, cooperation, and self-acceptance.

Understanding must be a constant and can only be found where there are no contradictions, making the pursuit of knowledge, ideals, beliefs, and rights the major red herrings, false flags, and massive deceptions of all idealistic thought. In addition to isms, our language again reveals the truth by calling these thing ideals —that is, imaginary rather than realistic conditions of existence.

The pursuit of knowledge, ideals, and beliefs makes happiness and fulfillment impossible simply because no ideal leads to realistic happiness and fulfillment or contentment.

Happiness and fulfillment originate only within the principles of the Value Perspective. When standing upon noncontradiction, honesty, and respect, only thoughtfulness, cooperation, and self-acceptance bring us happiness and fulfillment. Self-acceptance is the realization of contentment, the release from the need to convince the world of superior ideals and beliefs, and release from the pressure to materially fix problems that are the consequences of material thinking.

Reliance on the material way of thinking makes knowledge the precursor of chemical fixes such as cocaine, methamphetamines, and heroin. They provide the material person's fix. The socially approved but even more wicked and mean, is the ego euphoria fix. It is money, providing the power fix common to all empire builders.

Material progress is no substitute for happiness and contentment. The result is always the need for more, an insatiable desire that is never attainable by the methodology employed. And without understanding, there is no uniformity of thought and consequently no peace, merely the omnipresent need to fix, update, and expand power necessary for defense of the empires egos build. Material understanding of existence is impossible.

By accepting reasonless matter as the substance of our reality, Nature and God become our default way of explaining away the materially inexplicable—that is, materialism forces us to believe, to create an understanding of existence no matter how bad it might be. Material reasoning has no genuine foundation for eliminating absurd, evil, and simply wrong or destructive ways of thinking. If it did, these destructive ways of thinking would have never come to exist.

For material reasoning to be valid, it must include all ways of thinking and all manners of perception as reason has no valid manner of discriminating. The material solution is political correctness, the mandate of modern civil conduct. The modern political theory term for accepting this inexplicable miasma of irresolvable beliefs is *tolerance*, the word for admitting the continual existence of intolerance in our feelings or culturally speaking, no change at all.

As a result, reason is mired in a politically correct pea soup of rationalizations about existence that includes all manner of beliefs from evil to good, from concrete to ethereal, and from spirits to heavens and extraterrestrials. Nothing lies outside the scope of reasoning, and to trust its leadership is to be a fool, squandering the Value you are.

Likewise, the material intellect has no manner of determining what is important except power and the entourage of imaginary ideals, beliefs, laws, and protocols power employs to fill the emptiness of our failure to know and use the Principles of Existence.

Our willingness to waste in search of meaning verifies our desire to have genuine understanding—that is, to know the universe is rational. If the universe is not rational, all our efforts to find meaning and to understand, including belief and ideals driven actions are a waste of human resources. All debaucheries and opportunisms should be explored to the point of self-destruction to prove for the record their irrationality and the contradictions throughout the world and even the universe. Then we could eliminate the contradictions and build a truly civil existence.

Genuine civilization has to have a verifiable intellectual foundation and materially there is none. All we have today are beliefs, ideals, and laws. All are full of contradictions.

Actually understanding lies in the simplest of details and what is related next boggles my mind with its implications that, even in the simplest physical equation, big questions about materialism arise concerning the substance of existence.

By virtue of its motion, the energy contained in a material thing is determine by speed multiplied by its mass. This is reasoned material thinking. The physicist would write this as $e_{(energy)} = v_{(velocity)} x_{(times)} m_{(mass)}$ that is, $e = vm$.

The physicist would then test this experimentally, say with a falling apple (Isaac Newton) and find something quite different. $e = v^2 m$, that is velocity must be squared or multiplied by itself to get the real energy content of the falling apple at a given speed during its fall. I do not know why this is so except to say that velocity is a function of time and motion and when time or motion enters any equation it becomes evident material ways of thinking do not provide correct reasoning and reality becomes the arbiter of truth, not science. This suggest time is the critical and essential element of reality. The seemingly mysterious equations of provable science are simply the reports of physical experiments done by men.

This fact suggests something is wrong with our material vision of existence. It is unable to predict except by recall of past tests and that this material failure to predict is the reason we created science. All the mathematics of physics and engineering are simply finding the best mathematical equation that fits the results of arranged physicality.

Does this mean that material reasoning is wrong? It deceives you. It deceives you into thinking the facts of existence can only be discovered by white coated scientific experimenters who, in the largest sense, are unable to determine what is important and leave us without direction and consequently fawning to science in the material sense.

All meaningful advances in human thought occur in the mind of a single person and they occur because of attentiveness to real relationships, not the mysteries of science. Genuine science is the mind seeking to understand existence. Which means the real methodology must be the application of the principle of noncontradiction not the "scientific method."

We all seek genuine understanding unless we fall into the material traps of ideals, beliefs, and the validity of opinions all of which provide a sense of understanding. To be a professional scientist is to focus, to exclude much of the reality we live in and serve the interests of moneypower because even scientists cannot scientifically define what is important and find their own presence define critical tests.

Does this mean the Value Perspective is correct? Maybe. For why should personal presence affect other "material things" But nevertheless you have to prove the Value Perspective to yourself when the consequences accumulate to overwhelming argument. Then you will agree the Value Perspective works in every circumstance to benefit yourself and everyone. It makes the Principles of Existence our moral system and, of course, principles are universal. This condition is called understanding of existence.

Reining in Personal Understanding

Having an understanding of existence is important, but we need not squander our inheritance to find it. Understanding comes from study of thoughts just like Einstein's "thought experiments." But the self must be willing to eliminate ego formulated contradictory thoughts and consequential emotions and behavior. This process of eliminating contradiction is a toughie and requires a super important methodology, requiring strong internal objectivity and the ability to "eat crow," as the saying goes. It eliminates all conflict in the world if everyone did it.

Conflicts in relationships are the key. Anger is our response to contradiction—that is, anger identifies an assumption that need to be examined to eliminate contradictions. To resolve these issues, you must verbally discuss with the challenger or use "Einstein's thought experiments to the point of reaching rational understanding where you can actually see what is genuinely right.

Many times one will have to sleep on it to resolve the issue. I call this brutal honesty because it frequently requires eating crow to eliminate contradictions. However, this process takes very rewarding pressure-relieving intellectual steps away from beliefs or material ways of thinking and requires the staying power and unhindered (let your mind run) insight to reach the depths of thought resolution essential to what is right and noncontradiction.

If successful, your intellectual foundation has been rationally and automatically reset by your Value and you become a better person because you understand what is right. The vibrant Value you are, the part of you a material existence cannot admit, see, or touch, the part of you we have named creativity changes to make new and rational connections in your mind continued material thinking never provides.

In so doing, you will feel an euphoric movement toward understanding that eliminates the bad assumptions and changes who you are for the better. It is the experience of moving from an inherited material theory of existence to the Value Perspective where you become the active center of the universe, a legitimate particle of reality controlling your own destiny.

This release from ignorant assumptions is a very personal experience only momentarily painful as our learned and cherished material way of thinking (belief) is vaporized. In place of the assumed and demeaning convictions about a faked reality, a new, better, and freer self arises, having one less mind demeaning way of thinking.

Typically, leadership deceives us with freedom, justice, and human rights we must sacrifice for but can never truly attain. The freedom from contradiction spoken of in this book is the release from the belief mechanisms that exist to cope with ignorance. No sacrifice here. When material thought is replaced by understanding, each new realization turns out to be truth that sets us free. Freedom from ignorance and oppressive assumptions lack of understanding fosters.

The purpose of the mind is to deal successfully with reality. When we assume beliefs and ideals we guarantee divergence away from rationality in favor of imaginary and idealistic reasoning we will never attain because they contain contradictions. Here we can see beliefs and ideals actually prevent our minds from reaching understanding of existence.

The Principles of Existence resolve all the irresolvables and eventually lead to an understanding of existence that is wholly desirable or genuinely gratifying with no bad side effects. When one understands existence, one knows the formula of how to meaningfully accomplish gratification of self. This gratification arises from our relationships with others through satisfaction with our own genuine intellectual ability and growth. It also includes awareness of our contribution to a cultural existence that is moving to genuine goodness.

If we, in our gymnastics of "reasonable assumptions" include contradictions, we become self-destructive, moody, indefinable, unpredictable, and incapable of supporting actions that are consistent with our Value. This leaves us with inexplicable anger, the key identifier of having embraced a material perspective. Anger identifies a contradiction. Use anger to steer your search for exactly that which relieves anger, the resolution of a contradiction.

Anger and its permutations or sense of wrongness is in reality the only tool we have for identifying wrongness, and the Principles of Existence are the only tools we have for generating goodness. This flies in the face of all laws and commandments.

The illusions of laws and commandments are presumed to keep us from hurting (contradicting) ourselves and others. They are enforced with all kinds of power, and still they fail us miserably by misdirecting our thoughts to governmental solutions. These solutions fail to instill in our minds the self-serving Principles of Existence to guide our natural opportunism.

Commandments and laws, all of them, contradict the successful application of our own minds. Every law and commandment must have numerous exceptions to its rule, No exceptions needed for the principle of noncontradiction. To eliminate contradiction is to free all minds from the demeaning effects. Indeed, all Principles of Existence are universal, acting consistently throughout the universe to prevent demeaning actions and rationally define existence.

The disintegration of materially guided contradictory ideas in human culture is not instantaneous though. It takes time for contradictions to manifest their self-destructive nature through actions that reveal ways of thinking that do not support existence of the human particle.

Even quantum physicists, who work with incredibly small time intervals and with subatomic things they incorrectly believe are the workshop where our reality is formed, find it takes time for scientific contradictions (the collision of sub atomic things) to materialize into the nothingness they try to understand.

As each subatomic particle is accelerated and smashed into others, fragments appear and then disappear. Scientists name these fragments and then try to understand them, but they all disappear in fractions of a second. Why? It seems to me these subatomic things have left the atomic or real existence realm of predictability necessary to sustain real things. Regarding existence, time, that essential element of Value, is their enemy just as it is for us when we contain contradictory thoughts.

Likewise, we exist in a mega-time interval where slow-moving contradictory thoughts are moving toward their inevitable consequence: disintegration. Thus no matter how solicitous, erudite, professional, imaginative, or charismatic leaders are today, no leadership is genuine leadership unless it enforces the mandate of eliminating demeaning ideals and beliefs or contradictions across the whole social contract without exceptions. That is, from the pinnacles of imagined civilization to the bedroom, our successful existence depends upon effectively understanding and applying the Principles of Existence.

Exploring Hooliganism

There are many faked authorities, but there is no other genuine authority but yourself.

I like the word hooligan. Its usage is popular in Russian language propaganda, for it is one of their favorite expressions for nonsense.

Hooligan describes the intellectually insecure and malcontented pundits who would discredit what is said herein simply on the grounds of redundancy, errors of expression, manner of expression, or other superficial or even unrelated criticisms. In truth, these criticisms and character attacks are diversions that avoid directly facing the issue being discussed.

In tackling a subject as large as this book attempts, it would be foolish to think there are not a great deal of similar types of thinking, all centering on the same topic—that is, the faking of what is important. The genuine need is, to recognize that we are made of Value.

Grasping the concepts herein is a difficult task that has taken me about twenty-six years to accomplish. Many corridors of thought and word meanings had to be questioned, arranged, rethought, ruminated about, and restated as they reached the printed page.

The personal keys to unlocking so many conundrums are highly variable and very specific to each person. For this reason, many similar approaches to the same fundamental problems stand to reveal truth in the best way possible. I leave it to the reader to examine what is said when meanings appear foggy, off track, incoherent, illogical, or just plain nonsense. I leave it to the reader to read carefully and thoughtfully, to look at word meanings and read between the lines for unobvious meanings. I leave it to the reader to search for Understanding.

Materialism, Intelligence, War and Freedom

To believe is to admit we do not know the truth. This observation reveals the eventual end of material ways of thinking because following unprovable "truths" is, in time, always self-defeating. Beliefs have no intellectual foundation and are ultimately unsupportable. This is the genuine reason empires fall to internal rot as they always do.

If we use an incorrect perspective in our search for understanding, we have no option but to believe. In this choice to believe, we undermine personal rationality and base our whole life upon an indeterminably corrupt bag of assumptions, e.g., beliefs, ideals, and opinions. Having this foundation, reason is incapable of defining genuine goodness, so we created rationality and must continually try to define it as a genuine definition of goodness because rationality is impossible from a material perspective.

Crucial to our future is the matter of what is important. Always provable rationality demands a foundational or intellectual focus that is universally true. A material vision of existence has no such foundation and defines all materially inexplicable observations with beliefs. In accepting these substitutions in place of understanding, we find understanding of existence impossible. Consequently, we find reason and apparent rationality with no foundation and failing to create a genuine particle of existence. We fail because beliefs are not real and determine our false conduct in existence.

No matter where we look, Value is the force driving man and all things. That is, Value's expression is an internal happening, reflecting the gratifications you require for your existence. It is determined by what will gratify us and was incorporated in us at conception.

We are the Value first initiated by decisions of the ova and sperm to incorporate Values and form a new Value. It brings to our attention that awareness or consciousness is not uncommon but rather universal and something whose scope is defined by Value's need, not Nature.

Existence began back when the first atom joined with the second atom to form the predictable or rational reality of atoms and their compounds. To search in the subatomic field dominated by quantum mechanical theory is to look into a bottomless pit where predictability does not exist. This quantum (indistinct) focus forces us to probabilities while each of us is a distinctly defined real thing, a Value.

The inconsistencies between probabilities and distinctly defined Value can be seen in the predicaments of modern day medicine where percentages or probabilities supplant understanding and predictability.

In a material existence, Nature or DNA and God are charged with sacred or unknown responsibility, as matter has no reason to do anything. Materially, man's future is controlled by Nature, DNA, God, and something insecure egos call intelligence.

The conflicts or contradictions are monumental because each entity has a different purpose. But, by virtue of our intelligence and free will, we are assumed to be in control of our future. If Nature, DNA, and God are in control, why all the fuss about intelligence, free will, knowledge, morality, ideals, wars, and peace? Why all the laws? What an inconceivable mess!

If intelligence and free will are in control, why are we doing such a miserable job? Answer. Material ways of thinking that use force to elicit changes in a materially conceive existence—that is, material solutions with the incorrect perception of a material existence. It does not work!

A whole world of stupidity lies at this junction of nature, DNA, intelligence, free will, and God in a material existence. In fact there is a clear contradiction, as Nature, DNA, God, and intelligence cannot collectively be in control of our opportunism as purposes would be muddled (contradictory) and we would self-destruct in time.

This explains our continual turmoil, as nobody is in charge except the unseen and obscene agglomeration of money controlled by the occult and the events our governments pretend to control. A full exploration of our ignorant pot of assumptions has remained in limbo because material perception is incapable of answering basic "why" questions, and limbo serves the diversionary needs of OMNSWO.

In this ignorance we have madly lurched "forward" only to create a string of empires, including the United States of America, all of which use the same material ways of thinking full of unanswered whys. The resulting fakery of civilization has become so ubiquitous as to demand constant war. We call war's essential technology "progress," but reflection upon this progress says otherwise.

All the evils of modern human existence lie in the differences between reason and genuine rationality first properly defined herein. Genuine rationality is exclusively that part of reason actually supporting our existence. But in a material world full of beliefs, rationality is impossible to define without contradiction. As a result, we introduce beliefs and needed privacy to hide our inability to differentiate between what genuinely supports existence and that which we fake via the ego.

No matter how intelligent we claim to be, if reality should be thought of in an incorrect manner, that part of reason outside of genuine rationality will dictate the dominant, destructive fakery of civilization we are currently experiencing.

Faked civility (the world of ideals, beliefs, and opinions) only appears to support one's existence and has all kinds of bad consequences. For example, the USA fought a war for independence, and we fought a civil war presumed to hinge upon the elimination of slavery. Both are thought to be wars about freedom, but they were not. They were wars about the misdirection of certain material ways of thinking.

Freedom is not the issue. The termination of incorrect material ways of thinking is the issue. That is, no war where freedom is the focus will ever terminate bad, material ways of thinking. The popular issue is always preservation of freedom, a freedom full of contradictions and misperceptions that caused the war in the first place. In its true sense, the freedom argument plus privacy and collusion permits the holding of any manner of thought, opinion, and belief, including slavery, taxation and occult sacrifice.

Including the physical, economic, political, and philosophical aspects of war and excluding the purely self-defensive reaction, all participants in war are merely expressing opportunism consistent with their own material (private and deceiving) ways of thinking. Both sides reason or use the illusion of ideals that are impossible to achieve, and the only material resolution resides in the inescapable material maxim "Power makes right" underwriting all wars.

All war is the complete abrogation of our mind's ability to address the real problem, which is how we think or what we perceive as important. The answer reveals the contradictory nonsense of war. The real solution resides in recognizing the Value of which each of us are made.

When we look at the evolution of material thinking, the higher any person rates on current scales of intelligence, the further he will deviate from what is rational because he will be climbing the ladder of faked civility dictated by material perception and the consequential dependence upon coercion, force, and power needed to pursue the illusion of ideals. It is represented in man by the inception and growth of ego and the buildings we need to edify and enforce ego, the faking of importance.

Exposing Ignorance

Every way of thinking must have a foundational assumption upon which all conclusions stand. For the material perspective, this foundation is frequently God—that is, "In God we trust." Even though some people find this dependency impossible to accept, God stands as the foundation we Americans legally accept.

This observation includes all ideals, beliefs, and opinions, none of which can be tied to genuine goodness for self or the human race. None of them have any intellectually sound basis for what would be true rationality. All of them are a reasoned ways to make us feel better about our inability to understand in totality how material thinking drives us down a very bad road no matter what ideals and beliefs are promulgated.

With material reasoning we have chosen an unnecessary but inescapable course to build the most destructive and powerful war machines ever. It is a world based in ideals, beliefs, and opinions and, as a consequence, loaded with contradictions and massive power to defend the intellectually indefensible.

The growth of this power confirms the materially wrought and inescapably bad consequences of "Knowledge is power" and "Power makes right," both of which totally invalidate our litany of 'supposedly good rationales.' These 'supposedly good rationales' include freedom, justice, rights, representation, democracy, socialism, libertarianism, collectivism, and communism but do not necessarily include dictatorial systems.

With dictatorships it is possible to have governments approaching true goodness because goodness can be the consequence of a dictator who intuitively and intellectually follows what constitutes genuine goodness. They would be benevolent dictatorships that rule without the need for deception and hence have no need to be overthrown except by powers who want what they have.

In a materially conceived world, little knowledge brings what is genuinely good or bad to our awareness. Materiality is amoral, and any goodness derived therefrom is relative and transient because it lacks a reproducible understanding of what is rational. Assume a material perspective, and we get the world of today, which is dictated by reason to be politically correct and yet corrupt at all levels.

Trust is seldom, if ever, part of public discourse, because everything is conducted atop an inadmissible base of egoism supported by faked or politically correct illusions. The moral content of such discussions is secretly confrontational in nature—that is, they must be politically correct to avoid exposing the real issue, which is in some manner, a violation of the Principles of Existence.

In place of meaningful discussions, we are consumed with ideals, laws, economic theory, social theory, scientific theory, gods, beliefs, free trade, globalism, the stone and concrete buildings for the bureaucracy they demand, and the empire sustaining industries of presumed defense, which are thought to defend the whole system of governmental illusion or what ultimately turns out to be the falsehoods of freedom, justice, rights, beliefs, ideals, democracy, brotherhood, salvation, and all the isms of our existence.

We call the resulting dialogues "progress," but it is an empty progress whose illusions are made necessary by the need to divert our attention from material emptiness and resulting usury. The illusions have no sensibly good intellectual foundation, and for that reason the purveyors of progress must all resort to politically correct hype, glossing, lying, deception, intimidation, coercion, marginalization, and violence to maintain the faked civility they support.

These reasoned material ways of thinking are the destroyers of the human mind. Their effect is to stultify and even reverse personal growth, forcing us into an irresolvable conflict between faked civility (political correctness) and our Value's potential for understanding what constitutes genuine civility and progress. Genuine civility and true progress is the movement from material ignorance to understanding whose source is the Value Perspective and its Principles of Existence.

Jerry Hewes

Part 4 - The Examination

Unhinged Morality

Every one of us exists to gratify the Value we are. That is, we are opportunists, and for that reason genuine goodness is defined by the Principles of Existence that originate from the realization that we are and everything is made of Value. Any other standard, ideal, or belief is false.

This is the beauty of principles. They are universal and are applicable anywhere, anytime and you are the one making all interpretations and decisions.

All commandments, laws, protocols, and codes of behavior are control oriented, centralized, inflexible, and arbitrary in both their interpretation and application. In other words, you are never in charge. Never mind, though; go do your thing, and if you are never caught, you are free to continue, no matter what you do. Only the charts we focus upon are important. This is the world of today.

Every religious commandment is also empty of meaning and open to wide interpretation, permissiveness, and the misguided collusions of privileged classes working under the guise of authority, infallibility, and salvation.

Recognizing that no modern morality works, pragmatic egos (modern leadership) step in with their own realities and stretch materially reasoned morality to the ridiculous with ideals, beliefs, and political correctness. And now we have apparently moral demonstrations about global warming, racism, and economic disparities where there is a huge need to identify the full truth of what motivates people to demonstrate without the agendas and support of unearned money.

Examples of unearned money would be taxes, fines, stealing, diversionary financial advice, profiteering, bribes, contributions, skimming, tariffs, and all those other opportunities where accumulation of meaningful amounts of money are made possible by the seemingly insignificant or un-noteworthy size of hidden multiple thefts.

Are unearned money demonstrations spontaneous? Not at all. They express the constant pressure of the need for security in a material existence, the need for more moneypower by those who have already stolen their existence from us.

When demonstrations go beyond personal local issues it requires moneypower to pump up the demonstration machine. Unfortunately, this funding is the money separated from the morality of the Principles of Existence and has an agenda consistent with the unseen character of moneypower players.

This amoral money supports moneypower using the same methodologies and idealistic illusions practiced for thousands of years enlarged, refined, and enhanced through opportunities for widespread illusions manufactured through demonstrations.

The recipients of unearned money do not know that this moneypower is less than worthless partly because it supports them. But it is less than worthless because it carries with it the elimination of genuine morality earned by the producer of wealth.

We do not commonly see unearned money in this light because we think materially and can only visualize that money has no moral implications. But moneypower has no investment in free money, and thus the free money is used without regard for the Principles of Existence.

From such aggregations of unhinged-from-morality money, all the perversions of the world come into existence. From Stalin to Lenin to Hitler and now the United States where patterns of hard-to-stigmatize, hard to unmask illusory thinking seek to sustain and enhance the flow of unearned money.

It is unearned money making perversion and destruction of the Principles of Existence possible. For the networks and governments to which such sums accrue, there is only the faking of morality.

No person is entitled to a free ride in existence. Feeling this entitlement establishes a personal disconnect between a genuinely meaningful existence and a faked one and diverts people's attention to the cow instead of the garden and hay field where the work is done.

Because numerous people are in the business of collecting unearned money, we must have competitive efficiencies (faked civilizations) to create amounts of money worth stealing. This process consists of every imaginable corruption of our culture, including: the hurry syndrome or competitive efficiency, imaginary progress or charts, lies, deceptions, misinformation, diversions, omissions, secrecy/occultism, collusion, intimidation, and conspiracy.

"Progress" in this realm has nothing to do with personal happiness. It is created and managed within the fog of dishonest and disrespectful illusions such as progress charts or economic indicators, freedom, justice, honor, and everything else we are told we fight for.

To support this deception we initiate valor, courage, and honor the truly disgraceful uniforms of war and authority we hide our travesties behind. In a very significant sense these uniforms blind us by compelling all of us to support such nonsense to create even greater pools of amoral unearned money.

Despite the rhetoric, decorations, illusions, and hype, in a material reality there is no smart approach and no understanding of genuinely good morality. If we think materially—that is, relying on compulsion, illusion, and killing to coerce and pretend goodness, everyone is wrong, morally and eternally wrong! Material ways of thinking do not work.

If we intend to experience a life worth possessing, the Principles of Existence stand paramount. They originate with the observation that everything is made of Value.

Identifying Our Foundation, the Answer to What Is Important

The Value Perspective is unlimited in its scope and can be understood by any person who makes an effort to understand existence. The Value Perspective provides the opportunity for one to think on the largest scale possible by eliminating beliefs, identifying contradictions, and ultimately recognizing what is true through the absence of contradiction—that is, the attainment of understanding.

In time the Value Perspective will totally redefine human existence. This change is a consequence material thinkers cannot allow because it destroys their egoistic personas and their vague box of faked civility. This is the reason we are unable to reach our potential. Our reality is this false material perspective underlying every imagined solution to human problems.

When we perceive reality incorrectly, any reasoning (anywhere in the universe) will generate consuming perversions. They are the ineffective, misdirected efforts called ideals, beliefs, and opinions, all of which are the fundamental essentials of an incorrectly visualized existence.

In the greatest scheming ever, we have the following:

- A complete failure to understand. Consequently, we base our existence in countless assumptions that cannot result in anything more than temporary and isolated escapes from a destructive intellectual environment.

- We sacrifice for freedom but we are never free from responsibility to self which ultimately includes everything. Another example is justice. True justice is the absence of injustice. What we call justice is revenge. Revenge resolves nothing and adds to the stressful hidden emotions of cultural instability.

- The turning to probabilities—that is, placing ourselves on charts of hope, the only option available to ignorance.

- Ideals, beliefs, and opinions. We hope these foundational unknowables will help us elect people to represent us in forming a genuinely good government. But, our hope has not materialized.

- "Moneypower." This is the evolution of materially inevitable axioms "Knowledge is power" and "Power makes right," and the extensively faked dogma they require, including the US Constitution. In 1975, the US secretary of state, Henry Kissinger, said in an unguarded moment, "The illegal we do immediately; the unconstitutional takes a little longer" ("The New American," November 8, 2010). It reflects precisely how the Network or OMNSWO and moneypower views our government.

- OMNSWO: Old Methodology New Scale World Order. It is an in the background oligarchy, or conspiracy of world-manipulating wealth. OMNSWO's lifeblood is steering governments, commerce, loaning, interest charges, protection, printing money, credit, blackmail, enticement, and a learned understanding of the deceptions that divert our minds from their unprincipled actions. Sometimes their actions are fearmongering. Other times they promise progress and peace or illusions thought to ameliorate our fears. They say and do whatever it takes to get the control they want.

OMNSWO is now attempting to manage world commerce by creating an imaginary environment and legal framework that serve, more than anything else, its worldwide, long-term, insatiable need for unearned money.

This Network adheres to no principles and routinely employs all material methodologies, including deception, usury, blackmail, marginalization, murder, and the incitement of civil unrest, all as a function of the "Power makes right" axiom and their need for control.

Can we know this? The answer is yes. Here we must look to noncontradiction. There are two contradicting routes both known and experienced in our minds and culture. 1. That materialism and its corruptions are in legal control. 2. This contradiction does not invalidate the moments when our unknown indwelling Principles of Existence create the existence we sense as good which is most of the time.

The people who make up the moneypower Network are all but invisible, identifiable only by surrounding power, tight lips, and what they support. They are highlighted by hidden wealth initiating behind-the-scenes chicanery, and a laid-back or uncomplaining presence natural to exclusivity and overarching power. If it is important to their purpose, they secretly and indirectly control everything necessary to their purpose, forming and funding international organizations with indifferent officious names to legitimize intimidation of governments and humankind.

The axioms and dogma, of this moneypower we tried to defeat with our Constitution, have been addressed materially or not at all. The writers of the Constitution failed to consider the ultimately overpowering consequences of moneypower and used material solutions when material thinking is The Problem.

The illusions of government establishes the need for control yet do nothing effective to change the way we think to what is genuinely good. As governments exist today, their power actually is the abrogation of the duty governments have to be good; the total failure to know, proselytize, indoctrinate, popularize, teach, and apply noncontradiction, honesty, respect, thoughtfulness, cooperation, and self-acceptance for all its citizens.

Because of this, we get the following:

- An incredible sinkhole of what turns out to be legislated corruption, or, more specifically, unearned moneygrubbing, deceptively funded by us in the incredibly ridiculous belief that we have vanquished the moneypower evil descending from governments and above. As reported April 21, 2014, in the *Washington Times*, a study at Princeton University has concluded that democracy is dead: *"America is an oligarchy, not a democracy or republic."* But it has always been this way. What we are now experiencing is the maturation of this unprincipled moneypower realm to a level affecting all cultures.
- The resulting cultural distortions and the debt service that future generations will inherit.

- A leadership of faked moral goodness, whose competitive operating parameter is, in the full sense, the need to get reelected or influentially employed where unearned money flows to corrupt a materially conceived existence.

- Insecurity, with necessary compliance to moneypower. We seek pervasive intelligence or information and speak and use rationales of misinformation, deceit, and omission. The government monitors our computers, our telephones, our schools, our financial institutions, and much more. These avenues for the collection of information are perpetuated by our own government or other malevolent forces we have not been allowed to see. This information is used to initiate deception, marginalization, termination, blackmail or manipulate the individual, and eliminate threats to moneypower.

- The failure to observe the consequences of unearned money. There are no free rides. Everyone must earn his or her way. The existence of gargantuan sums of unearned money beyond even the scope of government has no good purpose. It is not ours to command. This is because it was accumulated materially—that is, stolen without the guidance of the Principles of Existence.

- Reason outside of rationality, directly, indirectly, and on the sly for the purposes of deception, control, and moneypower. All of this is wholly dependent upon knowledge to enact power and control, and to covertly subjugate our minds by deceiving us about what is right, and selectively omitting, twisting, or conditionalizing the Principles of Existence in our daily lives.

- The continual supply of unearned money, which is used to control an ill-constructed system according to some imaginary goodness actually unknowable to material man, where moneypower is the dominant power, an oligarchy.

- An educational system covertly dedicated by omission, hype, ignorance, and illusion to educate the workers for a system of money collection.

This is our system! All the perverse things that seem to have happened spontaneously, as a matter of supposed collective human will, are directly or indirectly instigated by large amounts of unearned money frequently working on both sides of a conflict to get what the owners of unearned money want. They have an agenda whose function and details are secret (occult), making even our Constitution nothing more than a temporary obstruction to making money. "Power makes right" is their operating system.

In all of this, no organization stands paramount demanding noncontradiction, honesty, respect, thoughtfulness, cooperation, and self-acceptance as a unit essential for genuine and meaningful understanding. The Principles of Existence remain unknown.

Our material existence is the game of unearned money and its ability to engineer control of the way we think. Everything is a matter of beliefs and ideals, while moneypower juggles everything for the purpose of more moneypower. We have falsification of goodness on the grandest scale possible.

Unearned-money materialists will never accept what is said herein; they can be identified by their opposition to or silence about what is said herein. The Value we are and the supporting Principles of Existence will result in the end of the unearned-money realm. Moneypower's power to sponsor seemingly spontaneously organized happenings that pervert human direction to the agendas of moneypower will fade as the Principles of Existence become our method of operating.

All the evils of modern culture are simply the negative consequences of living in a materially perceived reality. The Principles of Existence, which are natural to our bodies, are continuously suppressed and corrupted by material ways of thinking. Answering the question of what is important means changing to the Value Perspective. In time, as each mind begins to understand, it will permanently correct all problems.

The Theory of Matter

Being predictable, the universe is rational. Our lack of understanding is the result of seeking knowledge rather than understanding.

Knowledge suggests we must know everything. Integrating all knowledge to achieve understanding is impossible and cements us in ignorance. Understanding only requires we know the operating principles by which everything acts. If followed, the universal thought contained in a principle yields predictability which equals understanding. Principles create an understanding of existence, for they answer the question why. A principle's purpose is to serve Value and make it real—that is, containing no contradiction.

It then becomes our responsibility to make this realness worth possessing by employing these principles, which guarantee the greatest gratifications possible for a Value seeking gratification.

Materially, we imagine matter as having no reason for doing anything.

To accept the material interpretation of existence is to accept a reality in which rationality is impossible to define amid beliefs, ideals, and opinions. The consequential reasoning becomes unrelated to goodness, a function of ideals, deities, Gods and Nature. Or more accurately, a function of intellects with no genuine foundation.

Matter has no reason to do anything. Matter is only an imagined mental substance we have assumed to be the substance of all things in a universe into which we force our illusions of what must be.

As a result, we have to imagine life as containing nebulous qualities named spirit, soul, and ego, as well as intelligence and competition, to explain what a material reality and its necessary illusions cannot comprehend—its own lack of valid moral principles originating from the Value Perspective.

From a material perspective, we assume that an understanding of existence is impossible. To fill the emptiness, we accept knowledge in the place of understanding only to find our power of reason morally empty, incapable of creating the world we sense is possible no matter how much knowledge is accumulated. Having assumed a material existence, we have had no alternative but to turn to intimidating and coercive force, coupled with the illusions of ideals and beliefs, in the deceptive attempt to achieve false images of civilization that, in ignorance, seem so essential to our existence.

Having no alternative to material interpretations of existence we have:

- turned to imaginary freedom, justice, rights, with their glib and contradictory protocols;

- turned to deceit; appealed to ignorance with vagueness, misinformation, and misleading statements, impossible illusions, and utilized intimidation, force, ideals, beliefs, and spiritualism, revealing the abandonment of our rational potential and consequential inability to achieve the civility we sense is possible;

- rendered our intellect ineffective except through expressions of force, including intimidation, coercion, deception, and termination to achieve idealistic, faked, and impossible goals;

- employed self-destructive goals that are impossible to reach, as they are contradictory (i.e., inconsistent with reality, rationality, and continued existence)

An excellent example of the consequence of assuming a material existence is the ideal of freedom. Freedom is not universal and therefore not a principle. It is conditional and defined only as a whim of the intellect.

The first problem is food. We are all bound to the need for food, not to mention shelter and clothing. We must all work in some manner for these essentials. And we face issues such as killing, stealing, cheating, deception, usury, slavery, and so on. Are we free to do these? If not, who decides?

By our desire for goodness, we are forced back to this idea of government, with all the unfortunate, mind-demeaning trappings of materialism we wish to be free of.

In short, none of us can define this freedom unless we begin limiting our definition to exclude the contradictory parts, and ultimately the whole concept. The contradictions destroy freedom's ability to offer concrete meaning because the definition is dependent upon the speaker's interpretation and thus completely arbitrary.

Freedom is simply a way of appealing to minds willing to believe in something that promises freedom from responsibility, and most particularly freedom from the work of defining anything. It is a tremendous tool of illusion for egos who do not want us to think and instead to lead us to reinforce their illusions, the real substance of modern leadership.

Consequently, freedom is a sugar coating that serves the purposes of those who want to create intellectual diversions—that is, the materialists. In other words, the essential use of the word freedom (and all ideals) is for material exploitation. Ideals simply disintegrate on close inspection.

Justice is another ideal we should assess our use of in a materially conceived existence. In reality justice can only be achieved by preventing injustice. Any other interpretation is false as once an injustice has been done any effort to correct the injustice is itself the addition of even more injustice in the consumption of energies to restore something already lost. Justice is like freedom, a red herring for those who want us to fight for their efforts at material resolutions while they fail to think in a manner that recognizes the importance of the Principles of Existence.

Revenge is the typical and materially legitimate reaction to injustice. I say legitimate because revenge is a personal, timely, appropriate, thoughtful and accurate response. To give the power of revenge to God or the state is to make it ineffective for lack of timeliness, meaningfulness, accuracy, and the distortions of moneypower.

In the Bible it says vengeance belongs to God, and this is good advice to anyone who thinks materially because it protects the wielder of vengeance from the adverse consequences of inattentiveness to his own life including ignorance, thoughtlessness, and the reaction of the recipient of revenge.

To anyone who perceives people as made of Value, they see how apparent adverse events or injustice become learning experiences and use whatever emotive forces are generated to intellectually prevent the injustice from reoccurring in the future. This is the expansion of justice.

This means all of us need to know and apply the Principles of Existence daily and be able to understand the circumstances and appropriate ways of thinking about injustice. This is something we should teach our children, for to understand the circumstances of injustice liberates all of us from the destructive and consuming emotion called revenge.

Noncontradiction, honesty, respect, and thoughtfulness tell us there are no free rides unless they are gifted or stolen from others. Unearned money perverts the mind-set of its owners away from thoughtfulness and cooperation essential to earning one's way, to intellects having no foundation and fear-bound by the resultant need for control of those who threaten this kind of wealth.

Because they are a natural part of us, the Principles of Existence define goodness in every situation, and each of us personally has what it takes (Value) to understand and define these principles in every situation. People do not use this faculty because they have not been taught. We and our governments have failed to emphasize the wisdom inside each of us through the recognition of Value as our substance and Value's inherent Principles of Existence.

Governments do not think. Governments are always tardy, even when they are responsible for a crisis. Government and all its trappings are just an artificial, illusory creation engendered by fears from the wrong perception of existence.

Indeed, the complete story of justice is unavailable to the government. Justice is defined by all the events and circumstances of all lives currently involved in a situation, as well as historical happenings and perspectives and how they all come together at the junction of justice and injustice, something that is humanly impossible to administrate.

Assuming a material existence, every mind is forced to imagine such illusions, and it always ends in contradictory or destructive consequences. Freedom, justice, and everything else we accept as essential to governmental function are just myths. They are imaginary constructs of minds who think only of material advantage and overlook the fact that genuine change in our condition ***must be preceded by genuine changes in the way we think***. We must replace these illusions with the Principles of Existence if we want genuine goodness in our relationships.

Value is not a theory and neither does it employ materialistic ideals. It is a different way of thinking genuinely bonded with the highest expectations of happiness and contentment.

Any civility we think originates with material thinking is simply faked by compelling conformity to these attractive ideals. The pursuit of freedom, justice, and all other ideals, including capitalism, socialism and communism, is the demeaning of every mind in existence on all sides of every fence to narrow definitions that close the mind to a greater reality which is the admission that we have no clue how freedom, collectivism, or any ideals benefit us.

Goodness is resolved in the best manner humanly possible by employment of the Principles of Existence and ignoring any idealistic or belief based palaver. The Value Perspective and its Principles of Existence create a whole new world.

What Is Important

The ultimate life-expanding question is, "What is important?" Indeed! It is that we are made of Value, for if we are made of ashes our reasoning minds would have no purpose. Being made of ashes, each person must invent his own purpose, and universal understanding becomes impossible.

An understanding of existence that is universal in its scope is only possible when contradictions are eliminated. Contradictory thoughts have no positive effect upon our lives except to identify error.

We might think of ourselves as enlightened, but we are living in the epoch of material thinking, the Age of Reason and reason is totally amoral. It says that we are all born ignorant. The power essential to enforcing ignorant ways of thinking comes directly from material perceiving. It evolves to the completely amoral axiom of "Power makes right."

Collectively, we have to feign goodness, as our minds would be struck numb if we knew the truth of how we participate in this saga of deception, frustration, malaise, sorrow, slavery, and death, all in the extreme and all unnecessary.

In faked reality, everyone thinks in terms of ideals, beliefs, and opinions and unwillingly supports that indeterminably corrupt bag of ideals, beliefs, and opinions. When the fundamental questions are asked, we respond according to material experience and we are forced to say, "In God we trust," I don't know, or nothing at all. Genuine understanding is not available.

In a material reality, neither collectively nor scientifically does anyone have sufficient knowledge to determine the twists, turns, and interactions of the minds of amoral men engrossed in material interpretations of existence. The result is that any action and any position can be rationalized in any mind, and humanity gets the consequences of faked morality, whose civility lies in the realm of ideals, beliefs, or whatever moneypower and OMNSWO can summon.

We never try to determine what is important because in a material reality what is important depends upon which ideal or belief a person thinks is important. If we back up a step to see what underlies this situation, we see the material perspective as an empty bag filled with imaginary understandings. The amoral materialist has no verifiable answer, only the imaginary. He is incapable of visualizing any deeper understanding.

Only the Value Perspective tells us what is important. The Value Perspective says, "We are Value." This is what is important, for it defines human existence with meaningful substance, and finally, genuine morality to protect that substance: the universal master principle, noncontradiction, and its five defining principles as tools to define and extend this Value.

The question "What is important?" reveals the choice between the material perspective and the Value Perspective as the most important choice we will ever make. This decision determines whether we take our place among the legitimate animals of earth or are just another Cenozoic creature. A creature preoccupied with its own material ego and as a consequence, willfully and mysteriously destroyed by its own ignorance, rejected by evolution as unfit not by the environment but by its own choice.

Stepping away from Beliefs, Ideals, and Opinions Essential to a Materially Viewed Existence

There are two ways of visualizing human existence. One is the material theory. The other is the Value Perspective. Some more thoughtful individuals sense an existence populated by Values, but this reality goes unacknowledged in our educational systems because material thought is incapable of perceiving an existence where Value is the substance of all things.

Material theory is the world of today. We need to realize that material thinking is unacceptable in its consequences. It generates everything bad happening to us in the past, present, and future. Yes, everything bad! We need to reject it and change the way we think.

Accept that you are Value and find yourself immediately flooded with a permanent sense of meaning and purpose. The meaning or purpose we inherit is to gratify the Value we are.

Truly successful opportunism can only be accomplished through noncontradictory thoughts and actions–that is, the application of the principles named here.

The master principle of all things is noncontradiction. In our intellectual existence, the supporting principles insuring non-contradictory behavior are:

- Honesty: Eliminates deceit, which is always contradictory.
- Respect: Eliminates contradictions in relationships.
- Thoughtfulness: Essential for making everything work noncontradictorily.
- Cooperation: The root of happiness. The absence of contradiction in human ways of thinking enables trust and cooperative collaboration.
- Self-acceptance: Contentment or the absence of internal contradiction.

Noncontradiction, honesty, respect, thoughtfulness, and cooperation set our stage for the ultimate principle, self-acceptance. The integrity wrought by these principles creates a mind where all thought can be accepted and integrated into one wholesome being. The ultimate consequence is contentment, or cessation of the need to rape the world.

With self-acceptance, we

- build a permanent and realistic sense of meaning and purpose, being the need to gratify self;
- enable full use of our minds for their intended purpose of self-gratification;
- grow the ability to resolve any issue by our own thought process;
- eliminate the need to control our neighbors and the world;
- seek knowable goodness to fulfill our hearts and minds in totality;
- achieve an understanding of existence;
- find that ideals, rights, and social/economic systems of opinions and illusions become meaningless apparitions of egos and governments whose deceptions we no longer need;
- become the center of the universe and exercise the power to control existence to our satisfaction;
- find that genuine gratification can be ours through recognition of our position in the universe;
- find the confidence essential to eliminating ego and its expressions of faked self-importance we use to push away our ignorant neighbors we fear might see our ignorance;
- finally and most importantly, find the freedom to explore just how to enjoy our existence here on earth, especially through shared experience.

Jerry Hewes

Part 5 - Delusional Objectivity

The Old–New World Order or OMNSWO

Within the chaotic world of beliefs, ideals, and moneypower the ultimate evolution of materialism has formed. We are led to believe it is a combination of the force, ideals and illusions essential to complete security and world peace.

Complete security and world peace promises and demands control of everything, which in turn requires continuous skimming of unearned wealth for the purposes of control, security, and ego gratification. This promised security is an amoral collection of illusions, toys, people, prestige, money, and power large enough to initiate and control world-class happenings like war and globalism. It is the New World Order renamed to reflect its true character, the **O**ld **M**ethodologies **N**ew **S**cale **W**orld **O**rder. —OMNSWO—

To say we have a "new world order" is a gross misstatement. Throughout history, the material realm has been sustained by speaking obliquely, idealistically, and deceptively by faking, lying, and overlooking details and consequences. This old world order has simply expanded its size to become the "new scale" apparition, which smells, tastes, and acts just like the old world order.

Now, for the first time, this old "New World Order" or OMNSWO of material ways of thinking actually expects to gain control over the whole world through methodologies evolving throughout the ages and claiming to create a new world.

This power is above all governments and has no obligation to anything except moneypower and illusions required to make it work. This idea has gone way beyond the skill, resources, and mandates of governments. This secretive "New World Order" actually tells us our governments have been emasculated and are simply manipulated to the ends of OMNSWO

Much of what these people want to do has already been done without our awareness by using unearned monies, manipulation of government officials, and the subterfuge of speaking idealistically and obliquely while omitting specific details and consequences.

One issue with this world-control megalomania is, who is going to be the champion of this king-of-the-mountain game? Materialism predicts that there will be no absolute king. Instead, there will be a yin-yang war on a worldwide scale between the major players, whoever they are, and we will be the ones financing this wasting until the world wide money skimming empire-building mentality collapses because of the material scourge awakening arising on this planet.

OMNSWO (**O**ld **M**ethodologies **N**ew **S**cale **W**orld **O**rder) makes our illusions of representative, constitutional, dictatorial, and collective governments irrelevant, yet continuing the illusions will help OMNSWO's purpose by avoiding conflict with the tyrants of our time. Our Constitution is being turned into the manner of control OMNSWO wants. They are bringing the material power used to corrupt our existence nationally to a whole new level, a worldwide system of corruption where, as in the mafia, unearned money is the glue of their existence.

At this time, no mechanism exists to control OMNSWO's actions. They are in control and will remain in control via occult (secret and indirect) means because they have the money to buy anything they want, including revolutions and wars with preordained or managed and scripted outcomes, to serve their purposes.

We will get what they ordain, and they brag about this "New World Order" as an unavoidable certainty of imaginary material plenty for man. The continuing material maxims of "Knowledge is power" and "Power makes right" guarantee their success as long as we think materially.

Simply stated, OMNSWO proponents have unearned wealth beyond our comprehension and the resultant power to steer world events, which guarantees the success of moneypower. Their mechanisms for continued funding are already in place. They have learned how to skim unearned wealth both openly and at the same time secretly through our government, legal system, and with international trade agreements written by moneypower and pressured through governments.

In the name of education, our children's minds are being effectively educated for continued ignorance and the usury it permits. As moneypower's perspective is material, they use material conditioning to reach all their goals. Their ultimate goal is for the population to remain ignorant and subject to their persuasions and remain "useful idiots."

> Useful idiots is a term variously used by a number of historical authors to classify egos and naive minds that do not see the final consequences of what they proclaim and do. It is attributed to Vladimir Lenin.

Material methodologies will still create all the problems endemic to the way we think, and as long as we think materially there will be no solution to our problems. This is an open door to moneypower's opportunism. There is no genius, no new ideas except the new technological hardware and its potential for enabling world domination on a New Scale.

The battle slithers on today in the United States Congress between sub-world class leaders of capitalism and the OMNSWO proponents directing the sub-world class leadership whose success is actually essential to OMNSWO's old money skimming methodologies.

OMNSWO's morality is defined materially and continues to embrace the axioms of material ways of thinking. These axioms are arbitrary and demeaning to our minds, and for that reason they will ultimately fail, as all contradictory (mind-demeaning) ways of thinking in time do.

With unearned wealth comes irresponsibility. No person of incomprehensible wealth has skin in the game, and they care not what we do as long as they maintain continued skimming. For them it is a game, the only game and even outrageous amoral actions are moral if we are made of ashes.

The power that is essential for the OMNSWO apparition, as well as the myths of democracy, freedom, justice, etc. is made possible by aggregations of unearned money so large as to be able to shape world thought by controlling the media as well as any individual. They manage world opinion by funding illusionary idealistic charlatans, social movements, and, of course, the wars whose outcomes they manipulate through control of these dupes as their remotely directed personal marionettes.

Such events are funded and orchestrated from the top down by powers that have larger agendas and are working beyond the scope of immediate events and governments to bring us their new vision of old methodologies. OMNSWO, the new world order changes nothing except scale—that is, usury of the human race organized on a worldwide scale. For OMNSWO, there is no morality to replace the axioms of our material perspective, so, they must resort to occultism at the top.

To think that we are and everything is made of Value changes nothing except the way we think.

The Value Perspective requires a great deal of courage and this same manner of thought in all people's minds is the only manner in which trust can be attained. It means that when we come face to face with any person who understands existence, he can be trusted to do the right thing without being told or coerced in any manner. It is a brotherhood of mutual trust that moneypower will never understand and consequently cannot control. But, it means we must all think alike.

The Value Perspective actually accomplishes this without conflict between individuals or sacrifice of individuality. The Value Perspective is the intellectual pursuit of understanding according to the Principles of Existence. From a correct perspective all rational minds or minds free of idealism, beliefs, and consuming insecurities will reach solutions of integrity.

The Ego

Found universally, but most pronounced among leadership and professionals, materially controlled intellects are infused with ego. The ego is identified by its pursuit of unchallengeable and unsupportable ideals, beliefs, and the emotive volatility required for their defense. Egoistic visions are defended and promulgated as if they were truths except that real truths require no defense, just explanation and a lack of pretentiousness.

The ego consists of various combinations of knowledge, practiced faked civility, and an unassailable phalanx of beliefs and ideals. Because ideals and beliefs are sometimes not easily recognizable or challengeable, beliefs and ideals provide an almost perfect diversionary tactic for egos faking civility. Ideals and beliefs are easily molded and defined according to the intellectual whims common to egos.

Those who fall victim to the allures of ego experience the diversion and destruction that are natural to idealistic illusions. They seek but are unable to find rational fulfillment of their own Value as they are governed by ego's insecurities, i.e., the exposure of reality faked.

Embracing the ego prevents the application of the Value Perspective because:

• The ego is imaginary. It was first named by Sigmund Freud (1856–1939) to explain away the impenetrable core of fakery in some people's minds.

• Egos are self-absorbed in what insures their security. As a result we have false flag events, SWAT teams ready to break down our doors, drones to spy on us, the National Security Agency, the Department of Homeland Security, and other government agencies to monitor our communications and media. All major news outlets are silently manipulated by people whose egoistic lack of rational foundation is concealed in rhetorical idealism, legal obfuscations, intimidation, blackmail, and brute force power.

- Ego cannot accept the Value Perspective. Skilled in the fakery essential to material control, the ego cannot allow the perception of any other manner of thinking and will, by any means within its power, prevent the exposure of egotistical thinking as incorrect. Such exposure would destroy ego's persona.

- Ego subscribes to the power of unearned money and the control of realms made possible by enormous amounts of unearned wealth regulated by nothing more than material morality which is whatever anyone wants it to be.

- Such ego is not amenable to the friendly, informal, and increasingly detailed discussions with neighbors, friends, and colleagues where rationality and learning refine our minds and build the growing understanding and trust our adventure should yield.

- Lacking trust, ego must categorize or divide man according to probabilities, of people grouped together by ideals, beliefs, and opinions.

Here we can see the importance of Einstein's inability to reconcile the probabilities of quantum mechanics with our need to understand. Understanding requires us to think noncontradictorily— that is, predictably.

- Materialism dictates ego's purpose and methodologies. Ruling egos cannot allow others to gather together to challenge the ego's order.

Our mistake is to assume the ego is an indelible part of our psyche. While it exists in varying degrees, it is fortified and given power by the emptiness and ignorance of a materially conceived existence. Should the Principles of Existence of the Value Perspective become common to our cultures, the ego will disappear as it would have no function. In its place will be rational definitions of existence agreeable to and considerate of all people and thus generate trust.

Truth

In our fruitless material search for understanding, egoism creates the environment where debauchery and corruption are inescapable tools for ego sustenance. As a result, truth becomes inexpressible because it exists within a quagmire of contradictory thoughts sustained by inviolate egos.

Truth should never be an issue, but it is the consuming issue today. When we are born, our first growth is understanding with no intellectual component. But something happens to all of us as we begin growth of the intellect. Our materially based intellectual culture takes us away from the truth.

Children become so intellectually altered by material thoughts that they are compelled to form an ego. The only other defenses are silence and mental deviations. Having no intellectual foundation, ego's function is to gratify the self within an imaginary explanation of existence where we achieve existence by any means, especially fakery and compulsion.

With the many misgivings we feel about what our culture does, the failure to know what is important has been the formative essence of education. My observation is that education cemented its material focus circa 1970 with the changing of Personnel departments to Human Resources departments by our universities. *Personnel* contained the idea that we were people with an essence (Value) setting us apart from materiality. A *resource* is always something external to self and in this case simply named human.

Human Resources contains a contradiction in meaning. To be human is to be the thing gratified by resources, not a resource. This corruption represented a fundamental shift across university thinking to an official interpretation of man as a material thing. This renaming was the admission that even highly educated material intellects could not see outside the material box and that education had become the act of shaping us to fit the purposes of moneypower.

With that confirmation of materiality, we officially became a culture of faked self-esteem as well as hype and usury. In accepting the Human Resources corruption, we sacrificed natural confidence and its intuited morality (the Principles of Existence) for money and a competitive environment.

The consequence is the demeaning, desecration, and prostitution of self to something it cannot materially rectify, the self-destructive lead of the faking ego. The ego can only be dismantled by dumping our material perspective and replacing it with our own internal Value in the form of the Principles of Existence as administered by self.

Materially we get the world of imagined superior material accomplishment, the world of freedom, justice, and human rights. It is imaginary because there is no understanding of what is important. The arguments run all the way from altruism to I am stronger than you to my bank account and my powerful friends and nation are more important than yours, the natural dead ends of material thinking. It is the ultimate escalation to knowledge-based competition and power-brokered conspiracies.

Fear, arising from underlying ignorance of what is important, dictates that my school and nation are inviolate. We call this illusion nationalism and patriotism and they require our sacrifice. Both are illusions the OMNSWO order finds useful to divert our perceiving away from their underlying world-dominating scheming now called globalism.

By adulthood, the genuine understanding of infants and children is long gone, replaced by a patchwork of perverted material understandings of ideals, beliefs, false ways of thinking, and unreasonable expectations. The growing divisions of class and status result in class distinctions of two basic groups, the commoner and the professional, where each unit of higher or faked understanding is for some particular segment of our population and named "the professional." It includes politicians, lawyers, and doctors.

Professionalism is distinguished mainly by education. It consists of eliminating the gross errors of common material thought and replacing them with "scientifically" and "objectively" provable intellectuality.

I included quotation marks on *scientifically* and *objectively* because these claims are neither scientific nor objective. They find their definitions in material criteria and consequently are all underwritten by ideals and beliefs with little if any understanding of where they lead. It explains why the more sophisticated we become, the more sophisticated we have to be, the knowledge syndrome.

Despite its own apparent professionalism, education still has ignorance, beliefs, and ideals, and the same material assumptions and protocols about what is assumed important for its foundation. Outstanding teachers are outstanding because they intuit something is more important than curriculum. It is to treat students as if they are made of Value rather than something to be named a Human Resource.

Here is the truth! When we get angry, as when power rules over intuited moral correctness, our minds are telling us a contradiction exists. Anger is sometimes late to appear because illusions and its iterations require time to appear and reveal to our minds the underlying anger. But a thorough mind will uncover anger in time.

When anger presents itself, it then becomes our solution to identify the contradiction. Sometimes it can be a very painful experience to learn the contradiction is actually in the way we personally think. It busts our ego, so to speak, but really the ego needed busting, and we will be better people for it. After the contradiction is identified, it disappears without effort, as our minds gladly make every attempt to be rational and discard that which does not serve our purpose. It makes us better people!

Unfortunately in education, purpose is aimed at competitive advantage and illusive ideals, not our ability to identify contradictions and reach understanding of existence. Demeaning competition and ideals bring forth the growth of the ego in the form of prestige, wealth, power, and exclusiveness.

Material reasoning says power is not connected to morality and consequently, can be used for any purpose. Thus, power and exclusiveness always provide the opportunity for the occult because moral emptiness must be filled and a material existence has no valid morality to fill it.

When "Power makes right" is emotively processed, our sensed moral wrongness is a response of our Value. It is the violation of our unacknowledged noncontradiction, honesty, respect, thoughtfulness, cooperation and potential for self-acceptance.

The sense of wrongness is the need for all of us to build a self of integrity, a self in which all thinking can be integrated to form our integratable (noncontradictory) ideas into self-acceptance and consequently contentment and the genuine expressions of Value/self.

Yes, Value and self are the same thing, and to permit contradictions is to demean in some sense if not destroy the Value you are. What is claimed to be truth must stand upon this foundation, or it stands only as a deception and contradiction.

The Unknown War

We are fighting an unknown war. It is the war for our minds. We are experiencing the actualization of illusions made by men who utilize knowledge to realize the unspoken axiom that power makes all rules defining our existence. This is accomplished by illusion, deceit, omission, just plain lying, cheating, intimidation, and force, including blackmail, marginalization, and assassinations of those standing in the way of power's goals.

Everybody knows something is up and that so much is wrong, but we do not understand existence. Everything in this book is a restatement of human existence from a different perspective, with understanding as its foundation.

Perceiving the nature of Value finally defines what is important and names the Principles of Existence, giving us the solid foundation and the wherewithal, to understand the problem. We finally have the opportunity to give genuine, meaningful direction to human actions in the form of the Principles of Existence that exist to serve the Value we are.

The progenitors of OMNSWO have no morality except their self-serving illusions presented as the sterilized visions of what we are told we want. Actually, we do not yet know what we want, and OMNSWO capitalizes mightily upon this ignorance, enabling them to deceive us on the grandest scale possible... world control.

Oh, yes, science does such wonderful things, but material ways of thinking have brought us in a few short years to the abyss where the biggest failure, our extinction, is now possible, even likely. Without the Principles of Existence, the perturbations of power and the consequential calamities of technological applications make this possible.

Now, power comes to us in the form of governments, corporations, and other systems that generate unconscionable agglomerations of unearned wealth. All of them, including the OMNSWO vision, function according to perverted ways of thinking sponsored by a materially perceived reality.

Extinction is a severe assessment. It is indicated by the fact that an incorrect perspective will always result in self-destructive consequences. An incorrect perspective is inconsistent with continued existence as it contains contradictions. Thus, leaders define what we do as "progress" because the illusion of progress gives room for their egos and the faking of civility. We have made no progress toward a genuine understanding of existence or a rational peace except that the perversions frustrating us are driving more minds to express their Value by pointing to elements of understanding.

The Propagation of Mythology

In an incorrectly perceived existence, the smarter we think we are, the dumber we become. The more irrevocably committed we become while pursuing a wrong course, the bigger our collective ego. It is fatal to lack understanding of existence and goodness. It is fatal to combine mathematical probabilities with science, political objectivity, beliefs, ideals, and opinions that are accepted as progress. It leads us up the ladder of presumed progress until some probability fails and we are faced with an inevitability beyond the scope of probabilities.

The choices we make climbing this ladder of presumed progress are a function of the Value we are, but in assuming a material existence we do not perceive the Value we are. By clinging to beliefs we become the deluded ego and make wrong choices.

We cannot rely on probabilities at this juncture with existence, for delusion is ultimately fatal. That is, we must choose wisely all the time, and material guidance is a system that corrodes the direction of intuited good character. Material things have no reason for doing anything and provide no bona fide or verifiably good purpose. Whatever goodness exists comes from innate internal guidance living as it always does, in response to chaos.

If we are unalterably ego driven, with fakery of material goodness combined with the need to prevent exposure of our ignorance, we will chose annihilation over reflection and reassessment. All actions will be directed to preservation of the ego that is busy faking reality. The ego cannot allow the exposure of its ignorance.

All bloodshed is testimony to this amazing commitment to self-destruction at the hand of our own ego. The ego insists on creating a faked civility to gratify us in the absence of the Value we have not acknowledged. We must continually appease this emptiness through degrees of egoistic self-annihilation—that is, war and the decorations war bestows upon our dead bodies.

We are made of Value, to which ego is unrelated except destructively. To follow the dictates of ego is to leave Value unattended.

And so, leadership is a myth we follow because we have never realized that the material perspective is wrong and that our genuine course in this existence is a function of the choices our Value makes. Our choices are only twisted and perverted by the beliefs, ideals, opinions, and leadership made necessary by material thinking. Beliefs and ideals are then hyped by egoistic leaders who are incapable of relating what is important.

In our culture, the successful leader is the one best adapted to hype, the one most deeply involved in manipulations to hide truth. What this means is, the smarter the politician, the greater the divergence from the course that genuine understanding of human existence would dictate. In a materially perceived existence, the smarter we think we are, the dumber we become.

Science and Materiality

Despite its apparent successes, modern science is an abysmal failure. We stand no closer to understanding human existence today than we did thousands of years ago. We can now see just how close we are to self-annihilation via the technologies made possible by this science. These technologies are funded and directed by materialists who have no understanding of what is important. Even if we knew everything, this is incontrovertible: only the Value we are made of is important.

To be effective, true science must limit itself to investigations that fulfill our existence. Otherwise science corrodes and wanders to feed moneypower. But, of course, this is the culture egos feed within—that is, synthetic importance dictated by the needs of power in a material existence. With this model of science, we can leave no stone unturned before the competition gets there and, in reality, one of science's missions becomes hiding and obscuring of truth to frustrate the competition.

While we constantly grope for understanding, science can derive no understanding of what is important. It has no means to discover what is important. Because of this failure, we express these fundamental stand-in illusions that subvert human inquiry leading to understanding. They are:

- "Knowledge is power."
- "Power makes right."
- "In God we trust."
- commandments and laws
- sin and salvation
- beliefs, ideals, and opinions

These are the material inevitabilities. Their lack of beneficial consequences reflects and reinforces an assumption of a false and faked material reality that has no understanding of what is important. With these inevitabilities we have forged imaginary progress with all the ideals and words we use to describe what turns out to be faked civility!

- "Knowledge is power" yields the diversionary pursuit of often irrelevant knowledge.
- "Power makes right" exists to convince ignorant minds of power's invincibility and to convince materialists of the need for invincible power to enforce imaginary progress and defend it.
- Sensing that this was wrong, we invented "In God we trust." However, even those who speak of spiritualism, soul, heaven, and salvation are materialist. Their material focus is just another substitution of idealisms that reveal ignorance and failure to see that we and all things are made of Value for which no god is needed.
- Commandments and laws fill a moral intellectual vacuum— that is, they fake a morality unavailable to material thinkers. Commandments had to be identified and laws created to create the moneypower cash flow essential to what we have named civilization and which has now evolved to OMNSWO. Existing within this moral vacuum, it has turned to occultism to keep it participants under control.
- Because the Value we are seeks gratification, commandments name gratifying actions as sins, leading to a need for salvation. This is an attempt to inculcate guilt and subservience and cash flow to even more corrupt leadership egos having no solutions to the problems they name, the problems resolve by Value and the Principles of Existence.
- Beliefs, ideals, and opinions foster all the above because they have no verifiable foundation.

Predictability is the evidence that rationality governs all interactions in the universe. The universe is predictable except in the realm of man's material irrationality, which means rationality prevails everywhere except in a materially conceived intellect.

Lack of understanding gives religious believers room to create and seek escape with otherworld illusions. This false scope of material assumptions and beliefs, incorporated with the moneypower perversions of our intellects makes possible the biggest calamity humankind has worked to create, the complete loss of all rationality in the name of reason.

The sole exceptions to this direction are books and minds devoted to the search for understanding. They are not scientific works; rather, they are a search for truth that relies not on scientific method but upon the noncontradictory reasoning we are barely aware of.

The philosophers of the world have failed us miserably. Everything they have said is invalidated by their acceptance of a material reality. To the best of my awareness, the sole author who identified the importance of noncontradiction was Ayn Rand (1905–1982).

Literature, Noncontradiction, and Materiality

Great literature is great literature. It has no need to be updated. The great literature of Ayn Rand has led us to noncontradiction. The first and therefore illuminating investigation of noncontradiction was formulated by Rand, who wrote novels and informative books about its meaning and consequences. She recognized the incontrovertible substance related to human survival that noncontradiction contained.

Noncontradiction is essential to all existence. Intellectually, noncontradiction opens the doors to reexamine all aspects of human existence, including science, on a genuinely rational basis.

One effect of noncontradiction is to obliterate wasteful science. No, not to obliterate the inquiring mind but to obliterate all those who think the "scientific method" and its attendant elitism (white coats) are the solution to man's problems.

Noncontradiction works across the entire spectrum of existence. If a contradiction is observed by scientists, farmers, or scum alien beings on planet Zluck, no matter what the situation, no matter what assumptions stand in our minds, no matter where wealth or power lies, no matter what or whose focus stands paramount, something is wrong, absolutely and forever wrong. And guess what? The simple emotion of anger tells all creatures that something is wrong. Fix all contradictions in our thought process, and anger is permanently gone. Noncontradiction is our only source of truth. Its violation is the source of all anger.

Within this observation is the substance of all genuine progress for humankind. Anger offers us the opportunity to examine every relevant thought and action for noncontradiction of our Value. If we seek genuine, definable goodness, each of us must identify the consequences of what we think.

It is the Value Perspective (recognition of our mind's need for gratification) that makes understanding of existence possible, and understanding is what we should be seeking constantly in our learning process, our schooling. Noncontradiction guarantees the existence of all things in all situations. For man's intellect, it means we must employ and teach honesty, respect, thoughtfulness, cooperation, and self-acceptance the five additional principles that insure noncontradiction.

Really, isn't this what we want, for each of us to be able to identify wrongness in all its varieties? This process of identifying wrongness by eliminating contradictions leaves us with nothing but self-originating goodness—self-originating because genuine goodness has no other source. We are in charge of defining good, and noncontradiction and anger are the only intellectual tools that give us the opportunity to identify and eliminate the bad.

Contradictions are the products of minds who do not understand existence and have made uncountable assumptions by having no alternative but to believe, form ideals, and have opinions, as opposed to the understanding of existence available from the Value Perspective.

Consequently, our sociality is a mess, a hugely wasteful mess, whose most important mission of determining what is important has been diverted from fertile self-driven minds to corporate science, moneyed science, the secretive development of power and acquisition of money and of technology unrelated to noncontradictory thought.

Science now comes to humankind in a world-domination mode, where technology seems to make possible the control essential to those who see globalization and OMNSWO as the future of man. This is a future in which the blend of confidence and narrow-minded, statistically driven, and still fundamentally ignorant egos provide hidden control necessary to secure their vision.

For moneypower, contradiction is a meaningless word. Its actions are driven not by any realistic concept of human existence but by their need for money, power, and influence to accomplish their goals made necessary by their egos' faking of existence. All this happens because they fail to determine what is important. Their fundamental desires are to make their dishonesty quasi acceptable to us in the form of ideals like freedom, justice, globalism, and peace, all of which require the sacrifice of our minds.

Peace

Noncontradiction tells us that peace is only possible when everyone has the same foundational thoughts; then we, every person in the world, can cooperatively work together with trust for the same purposes. Anything less and we will always be divided with and separated from our neighbors. It is that simple. This means all of us must have the same view of existence, and the only view that is compatible with all people must be noncontradictory.

The correct view is that all people, including you and me, are made of Value, and every detail of our existence is governed by how well we apply the Principles of Existence, beginning with noncontradiction. It is what our minds are made for.

This writing carries no imprimatur except that of being human and consequently expresses no ego-driven agenda. My wife and I are farmers, first and foremost, with a very small wife-and-husband operation. We keep to ourselves, appreciate and enjoy our Value based environment.

We are introspective, grassroots people, with family, and we are what so many groups falsely claim to be when they're looking for money and allegiance to their quest for ideals and power. We live the Value Perspective daily. It is clear to us its application will reorganize cultural and social relationships across the board.

As the Value Perspective undermines all egos, countless naysayers in high positions will argue the claimed impracticality that such reorganization requires. This is plausibly true when one is so far removed from the truth. However, their real fear is exposure of having no genuine foundation.

I rely on clear logical thinking to give you the opportunity to reformulate existence in the manner that rationality requires. This is exactly what peace requires. What our minds accept as truth determines everything. Are we forced to rationalize for imaginary utopias, or does the rationality of Value stand paramount?

No corporate or educational science is responsible for my assessment of existence, and for that reason my assessment of truth is validated exclusively by rational or clean, uncomplicated thinking.

Our critical insight and reflective thought have identified no contradictions within the Value Perspective. With this perspective comes the Principles of Existence and the acceptance of a totally respectful opportunistic creature named man governed by these Principles of Existence. That's it! There is no need for any more intellectual junk in our existence.

The atom is the smallest unit of Value. The periodic table of elements suggests something like 118 differing elementary atoms. Despite our being able to smash these Values, they are the smallest units of *predictability* or things made of Value. Anything smaller requires actual smashing of predictable things and we enter the subatomic or quantum physics realm where probabilities rule.

Above the "probabilities" level or at the atomic level of thought, we get about 13,500 possible combinations of Value in just the first round of compounding Values (atoms). Going one step higher in the compounding of Values, we get something like 182 million possible combinations, and this is only the second rung of an broad and tall ladder of elemental compounding of Values each of which creates new Values *predictably*. This is where our truth is found.

Then the modern or corporate scientist stands before us, telling us he has the only answer, a probability. The catch here is probability. No one standing before a scientist is a probability. We are collections of all included Values working together to form one Value, the self. The self has specific needs, the consequence of innumerable smaller Values working with common purpose to form the Value of you. You are not a probability, and to treat you like one is abominable for those who claim science. Probabilities or percentiles are a manner of thinking necessitated by ignorant material assumptions. They are for Las Vegas and quantum physics.

Each time elementary atoms join with others, they do so according to Principles of Existence. In so doing they form a new Value or compound that joins and works together with other compounds to form even more Values until we get humankind. (No expressions of Value, no humankind.)

Existence is that simple, except that materially speaking we think "atoms," and then we jump contradictorily and absurdly to the conclusion that these things have no Value gratification and consequently no reason for doing anything. The truth is, there is nothing more rational than the actions of Values (atoms) and their compounds. They act with 100 percent predictability. Our whole universe stands upon this truth.

Jerry Hewes

Part 6 - Pointing the Way

Who Is in Charge?

We have been led to believe that we are inherently defective, that we are bound by original sin and ignorance, or material contamination, that understanding of existence is impossible and can only be determined by proper authority.

The materially focused human race has no convincing argument countering this assumption. Consequently, we have gurus, shamans, priests, ministers, doctors, scholars, psychologists, psychiatrists, social scientists, statisticians, political and economic advisors, and lastly politicians, dictators, and monarchs. They all depend upon the assumption that man must be governed and must seek guidance from or be controlled by some supra-personal being for which the speaker qualifies.

This is ridiculous. Who sets the standards we live by? And, if we set the standards, who is in charge? Representation is currently our last ditch effort to formulate governments we could accept by willingly thinking someone could represent us. It seemed so great that we could confidently will our self to others and painlessly create a government of freedom, justice, and goodness the world needs.

Yet, we cannot name a single person who truly represents us. In fact we don't even know where we want to go. There is no body of collective goodness arising from assemblies created through voting. Democracy is just the biggest diversion possible in the evolution of material thought where competition controls our material intellect's "greatest invention," the illusory democracy.

This competitive way of thinking ultimately provides total destruction of all human goodness in that red push button moment of presumed material superiority. Its only goodness is indwelling goodness we don't know how to name or sustain. It is carried forward by people who intuit what is genuinely good. It has no formal means of growth. It is being perverted by materially focused ignorance or egoism and moneypower.

There is no substitute for rigorous examination and reexamination of what we think. What we think is a function of the Value we are unless we let a politicians form our vision of existence, for this is what they do.

Forming our vision is what our minds are made for and the assumption of a material perspective has prevented all minds from reaching understanding of existence because... material things contain no reason to do anything so... we select politicians loaded with all kinds of contradictions that will never be resolved by the political process.

The absence of understanding and abdication of personal power this material thinking guarantees, is the working substance of all our social confusion, frustrations, self-destructive delusions, and personal failures. It is a material thinking problem with no material solution.

Welcome to the "New World Order" taking control today. OMNSWO is a solution that is just more of the same methodology on a larger scale and consequently no solution at all. One consequence of this perversion is diversion and delay from recognition of the evil nature of materialism.

Most of us believe we live in a material existence and yet, materialism is the unrecognized cause of the meaninglessness we continuously try to escape by creating ideals, beliefs and wars or material solutions. We assume these wars will install the ideals, confirm beliefs and cause social corrections. Have they?

By assuming this material existence, we have placed our ability to be rational in a box of incorrectly defined choices or the hyped ideals and beliefs essential for egoistic and faked leadership. As a result, we are the ignorant ones who would love to enjoy the fruits of total rationality but cannot because it is impossible to define meaningful goodness without a correct intellectual foundation. The result is monotony and boredom, the chasing of entertainment, and a sense of futility.

Recognition of material failure stands as our only potential for genuine success. But there is no escape from materiality unless the Value Perspective replaces our deceptive ways of thinking.

We strive for goodness. Everything we do seeks goodness in a fight to overcome ignorance and the evil inescapable in a material world. *We must recognize this utopia hasn't happened. We have failed to this day because the material perspective has prevented it from happening.*

Regardless of our material status, *genuine goodness originates with the individual. From nowhere else does a culture of genuine goodness originate.*

Are we born ignorant? No. Our intellects are created *undeveloped*, but our bodies are just fine. Mothers, fathers, and newborns know what to do even without words and we survive despite intellectual ignorance. Then we begin to generate intellectuality whose purpose should be to enhance the gratification of the Value we are. If we assume a material existence, it is at this juncture with reality where ignorance thwarts understanding and we must begin idealisms and beliefs in search for understanding.

It might seem natural to assume a material existence, but the reality is material things including gods have no reason to do anything. By intellectually accepting an amoral material theory of existence, we jettison the perception of our Value and use reason anyway we like. The result is a mix of rational and irrational material concepts proportional to how well we intuit our Value.

Materially, there is no foundation for intellectuality because gods are just the magicians of material realities we want to escape from. That we are made of Value means we are real and take action to gratify our Value here on earth. Perceiving we are the source of actions puts us in the driver's seat.

In a materially wrought culture there is no intellectual foundation except the commandments and laws hiding our ignorance and creating the anger and frustrations that build hate, retaliation, retribution, and vengeance.

Failing to discover this falsity of self-destructive material reasoning forces us to repress anger natural to material contradictions of self both physical and mental. This is the unbridgeable disconnect between material and Value perceiving. Anger is for our benefit, the identifier of contradiction and to suppress anger it is to commit one's self to endless and ineffective idealistic interpretations of existence.

Pent up outbursts of suppressed anger create shootings, demonstrations, domestic violence, and all violent force against others. In ignorance, hidden anger is used to incarcerate or isolate individuals and even nations in the name of imaginary justice, rights, and freedom.

There remain however a whole lexicon of material insults we accept and use regularly including nearly all laws and protocols of law enforcement. Unfortunately, to remove anger resulting from these insults is impossible materially speaking. They represent the control they say we cannot live without. Thus their reasoning is unchallengeable in their minds.

This failure to recognize that we are way off the track of goodness is the reason the intellectual leaders of our supposed civilization are now silent about the causes of violence and the reason anger builds to violent outbursts when imagined realities do not happen. As a result we have become a nation where futile shootings and legal actions both fail in their intentions; the results of thinking materially.

Within the Value Perspective, anger and violence are used to identify that contradictions exists. Then we use the intellect to identify contradictions. Once contradictions are identified, our minds automatically eliminate them. Gone are vitality wasting anger and the need to save the world from anger inspired contradictory illusion with its need for aggressive control. Our Value Perspective creates peace and vitality within us.

We have recognized ignorance since our time began with the universal perception that many things cannot be explained by material explanations of existence. They are frequently called love, spirit, intelligence, freedom, justice, the word of God or vengeance, and imaginary rewards for sacrifice.

These became the essential elevating parts of our sin and salvation story. But it necessitated love, spirit, intelligence, and the love of God to make existence quasi-understandable with hope and salvation the carrot on the stick.

Seeking knowledge was the natural result of accepting a material existence, but there is nothing more destructive than a mountain of knowledge built upon a fundamental misperception of existence. It makes the "knowledge is power" syndrome our reality not our salvation.

Sigmund Freud identified the ego as the explanation for the inexplicable and destructive selfism created in people's attempts to understand existence on top of a foundation of inescapable ignorance.

Ego is macho man, the inadmissibly faked savior mentality. Collectively, ego comes to us as the overwhelming authority of unearned money, governments, and the secret force of religions and idealists who, by virtue of their authoritative position, must act upon a foundation of ignorance about what is important.

Those who prattle material solutions to human problems must substitute illusions (ideals and beliefs) for genuine truth. The result of this substitution is the frustration of man's mind at every turn, because these substitutions for rationality are not only unrealistic to achieve but also diversionary from what is possible. They are destructive and wasteful of our emotive, intellectual, and physical strengths.

The inescapable result is a materialized culture with corruption at every turn, in every nook and cranny, behind every door. Modern civilization is a jaw-breaking, tooth-smashing, blood-drawing hit in the face, an insult to all sensitivity, knocking out our eyes and diverting all minds from the essential quest, which is to understand existence and consequently act in a manner consistent with existence.

We must see how badly material perceiving has served us and recognize we have made a very bad mistake. The assumption of materiality has made us unable to consistently make those decisions that genuinely gratify our Value. Instead we are exposed to outrageous risks.

In recognition of this error, we now find that genuine progress is tied to changing the way we think to the Value Perspective and application of the Principles of Existence.

Jerry Hewes

Understanding

Is understanding of existence possible? Absolutely, but not from a material perspective. We are not made of matter. Matter has no reason to do anything, and should material thinking actually become immutable law, existence would vanish as we self-destruct in a phantasmagorical orgy of exploding and imploding opportunism, perhaps much like a nuclear explosion or a pervasive, incurable mind rot. This is the inescapable future of man's material way of thinking, the direction we have accepted as normal because the material perspective has denied us understanding of existence.

To be sure, I am the egoistic authority on nothing, for I am not a philosopher, scientist, professional, political scientist, or elected leader. I am just a farmer who has done a lot of thinking and rejected contradictory ideas because I don't want anger in my life.

In my mind rationality stands paramount as the manner of acting for everything in existence. Take away rationality and nothing will respond sensibly to anything except in reaction, and existence dissolves to meaningless nothingness.

Existence makes perfect sense to every animal. No animal has any problem with understanding except man, whose materialized intellect stoops to manufacture faked civility. The animal trapped in ignorance is the animal seeking knowledge as the antidote of ignorance. We already know knowledge is essential to power. Power's function is to control and control means man is not his own master. Still to be realized is that understanding is the antidote of ignorance.

The historical and current solution to this ignorance or failure to understand is democracy. But because of material methodology rather than changing the way we think, democracy included unearned money and its need for power.

Unearned money is not an evil focal point but it should be. The first action of unearned money is collusion and conspiracy. In its highest evolve sense unearned money has to create occultism, the fountainhead of sacrosanct illusions OMNSWO must have to solidify, obscure, control, and "dignify" their unacceptable purpose.

Their purpose is the subversion of any or all governments to their needs by bribery, blackmail, and obfuscation of their intent. Their methodology is to include, in all governmental action, rationales deemed essential for the security and control of OMNSWO.

OMNSWO does not have the understanding of existence our minds need and find its substance in illusion and material actions. Their occult happenings must be hidden because of repulsive assumptions and suppositions about existence, including our need for sacrifice, control, and appeasement that must be dignified by sacrosanct illusions to pass before gullible (material) eyes not meant to understand.

The essence of occultism is not linked to the Value we are in any way, but on close inspection there are varying degrees or elements of occultism in many manners of material thought, including socialism, collectivism, communism, monarchs, capitalism, democracy, all religions, conservative, and liberal thinking. In every one of them there exist the inadmissible black imaginings of human nature, such as evil, secrecy, and sacrifice for control by imaginary gods of what turns out to be nothingness.

If we can accept this reality, the question becomes, why the occult? In every case, it is the rational emptiness of a materially perceived existence. This emptiness is guided only by contrived morals, forcing our minds to create a synthetic understanding of existence whose deepest unstated ideals must be kept secret. It plays right into the hands of ego building.

That is, we will accept even imaginary understanding to fill the material emptiness. The few who are agnostics and atheists choose to leave all the unanswered questions unresolved because they see the horrendous consequences of following ideals and beliefs.

All ideals and beliefs deny the ability of the mind to achieve understanding. Such lack of understanding is the demeaning of the whole human race to self-deluding destructiveness. We would even name lack of understanding (ignorance) evil and occult if we could comprehend its total consequences in our material culture.

Because we have been indoctrinated since childhood in material ways of thinking, including ideals and beliefs, materialism dominates our lives. Are we capable of change? I have no choice but to leave it to you. My only choice, and it was an imperative choice defined by the Principles of Existence, was to offer these thoughts to you.

It makes no sense to think there are aliens here on earth. With what we know about the dimensions of the universe and the nearest possibly inhabited planet, coupled with Albert Einstein's proven postulates relative to travel in the universe, **an alien presence on earth is impossible**.

Finding himself driven into a self-created quandary in subatomic material thinking, Einstein and others created quantum physics [indistinct mechanics] to account for the apparent nonsense of this atomic deconstruction. Einstein hated this insight which exposed a realm where conventional material thinking fails. As a result, science then turned to the application of probabilities and became indistinct.

In short, probabilities (percentile groupings) tell us nothing about who, what, why, or condition. Be it subatomic physics or our bodies, probabilities define nothing except statistics. The material exercise we call science is completely unable to visualize our comprehensive need for understanding (predictability) or from where understanding would arise. This scientifically inadmissible knowledge dilemma leaves the door wide open to reveal the Value interpretation of existence but material thinkers will never pass through this door.

As it has no genuine intellectual foundation, modern objective thought has no ability to determine what is genuinely important and relies instead on beliefs, ideals and the supernatural. Thus importance on earth is determined by material needs and illusions, not Value. Our direction is in the largest sense controlled by funding or the money flow of OMNSWO operating behind and above closed doors. Their master tool is the manipulation of those who claim to represent us in government.

The "authoritative" nature of science is made necessary by the fact we have failed to utilize the Value Perspective and gained the resulting understanding of existence and authority to act. Put material probabilities and understanding in a side-by-side test, and probabilities become totally useless. Modern science, knowledge, control, moneypower, statistics, and their included but inadmissible ignorance bring to us the egos, the fakers of material goodness including OMNSWO as the fundamental reason we do not get along with our neighbors.

Should any alien culture achieve a work-around of the impossibilities of interplanetary space travel and contact us, they would not subject themselves to the self-destructive nature of material perceiving. They would recoil in horror at our primitive condition and depart immediately.

They would not seek all the details characteristic of knowledge seekers in that scientific or failing attempt to understand. Aliens would see a few key characteristics like the pursuit of freedom, justice, and human rights and depart immediately as they have understanding of existence. They use the Principles of Existence.

Only a culture thinking in a noncontradictory way could evolve to the extent necessary to contact us. The presence of evil in alien creatures is a myth. Evil is self-destructive and consequently self-limiting. That is, evil cannot be, for it will in time, such imaginations will self-destruct.

This vision of evil exists at the expense of our imaginations where contradictory thoughts can exist side by side without discrimination. The substance of evil resides in materialism, ignorance and our failure to discriminate. The ability to discriminate is only made possible by the Value Perspective, the Principles of Existence, and the understanding that follows.

We think evil simply because it is one popular material diversion from what is important. Alien evil and evil in general is one perception we need to abandon if we expect to save ourselves from annihilation and become enduring members of the universe.

Value is the substance supporting the initiation of all action by everything in the universe. Spirits, angels, ghosts, goblins, ghouls, fairies, witches, wizards, devils, robots, and all the other imaginations evil and desirable have no birthing process, no substance, no rationales, no futures to support their existence in a universe made of Value.

The idea of alien presence is spoofed up by egos in and out of government who think they need the illusion of something more than what they are. The perpetrators of alien invasion panoramas do not realize critical thinking, from the Value Perspective, exposes the material power structure's need to create a faked evil-alien fear driven happening, to make their mechanisms of control seem necessary.

What brings all this thinking to conclusion is the realization that there are no free rides in existence, most especially for imaginary creatures. No matter what, every "thing" must do what is required to sustain existence—that is, the securing of gratifications essential to happiness and contentment. If any "thing" does not pay this price, it ceases to exist. I have yet to meet a ghost, spirit, or space alien in my entire life. Consequently, I am a strict realist.

It is here we see the tenacity essential to survive under the most trying conditions, and the power of cooperation and self-acceptance in the vision of a better existence. Those who follow actions called sacrifice and sacred honor are participating in acts for which honor is the stoical silence given to cover-up illusion's need for deception.

Understanding is the antidote of ignorance. What currently makes understanding an impossibility is our incorrect perspective. Obviously, no life-sustaining truth can be identified if our perspective does not correctly represent reality and, with our current twisted material mentality, realism descends into whatever debauchery, including occultism and evil that is indicated by resulting frustrations, lack of meaning, and imaginations.

Imaginary and limited understandings are laced with the poisons of beliefs where each of us creates a reality that secretly does not agree with our neighbors. This cultural dissonance sustains competition, egoism, arrogance, divisiveness, cultism, nationalism, government, democracy, war, and points to extinction as no militaristic society has survived its origins.

We now live in that time period between the initiation of contradictions and experiencing consequences. This period is prolonged by the actions of the genuine goodness of Value inherent in every person.

Understanding and separation of this dually driven reality is only discovered by the Value Perspective and the rigorous employment of noncontradiction or the Principles of Existence. Contradictory ideas cannot be integrated to form understanding. Noncontradiction is our first intellectual requirement after we discover we are made of Value because the stupidest thing one could do is contradict one's Value.

What makes noncontradiction so meaningful is that all thoughts deemed noncontradictory have passed the test for incorporation in your manner of thought, your persona, and contribute to, rather than conflicting with, your Value.

This understanding is naturally the same for all people, and the deceptions essential to all material ways of thinking are replaced by shared and cooperative thinking at all levels of thought between Value Perceiving people.

The Value Perspective yields the recognition that all people's thoughts are essentially the same. Personal gratification of Value and the Principles of Existence should always dictate everyone's future.

Noncontradiction creates integrity, which is the integration of all thinking leading us to understanding. Because we now recognize the nonmaterial nature of how we are gratified, the need to rape the world, presently hyped to us as progress, no longer exists. We can *self-accept* ourselves as legitimate universal particles acting and reacting in every way to gratify the Value we are.

Opportunism

Opportunism has some bad baggage associated with it. This is the direct result of thinking materially. Material interpretations of existence have no effective morality and allow opportunism to run without restriction creating every imaginable perversion of man's thinking including the occult. Occultism is the ultimate act, insuring in the materialist's mind, fear great enough to guarantee submission. Look for closed doors.

In our society, ritual sacrifice is also commonplace in the form of taxation, law enforcement, and military service. That forced conformity and service is done openly and justified by various idealistic illusions does not change its nature. It is sacrifice or the demeaning of our thinking faculties (occultism) that sacrifice forces us to endure.

Militarily, the word honor is sacred. But I have a problem with sacred honor. For example, in WWII honor was deeply embedded in the Japanese military as well as our own. What honor is there in manipulating (forcing) innocent people into trained warriors to kill and sacrifice for some ideal, no matter whose side they are on?

For the Principles of Existence and the person they create, opportunism is the natural, normal, and morally ***unexcelled state*** of our minds. We are not regulated by laws and commandments but by the Principles of Existence, our intellectual guidance system. We recognize the greatest gratification of self possible through adherence to them.

Of course this is counter to the way material thinking has mummified our minds. Materially, opportunism is a measure of scathing moral rectitude far beneath godliness yet essential to material competition. It's that old "necessary evil" contradiction. This is another of those hogwash illusions. Were it not for opportunism, we would all die, and quickly too, as everything we do to sustain our bodies is opportunistic, even breathing.

Morality is the nitty-gritty of opportunism. With materially created laws, ideals, and commandments, opportunism must be evil. Otherwise materialists would have nothing to regulate. From the Value Perspective, opportunism is essential to our existence and is morally shaped or guided by the Principles of Existence.

Corruption

Fighting corruption is useless. Leave it alone and it will expose itself. Corruption is both natural and normal to any mind that thinks materially. Only a change in perspective can remove this consequence by replacing material thinking with thinking that originates from the Value Perspective, the recognition and employment of the Principles of Existence. Anything else will ultimately result in corruption and the demeaning of existence no matter whose material morality we pursue.

Governments, Laws, Religions, and Theories

Governments, laws, religions, philosophies, and their theories are the sand castles of material thinking. They are necessitated by our failure to perceive the Value we are and to employ the Principles of Existence that would result. Our natural opportunism would be successfully controlled by the application of the Principles of Existence if we knew what they were and how they benefits us.

Using governments, laws, and religions is something like hiring a blind carpenter to build a house. No! It is really much worse. A blind carpenter has lived in a house and understands the requirements of a house. His apparent problems cannot be solved by legislation, commandments, or any ideal, belief, or opinion, but he understands the way.

Indeed, his perspicacity could even be enhanced by his lack of vision. He works by experience, careful noncontradictory thinking, and refined touch with no distractions. His final product will be an enhancing part of his survival because of the protection the house offers and the immense gratification of his Value that completion of such a project would suggest. He will fail on color selection, but cooperation can solve this problem too. And, of course, natural colors are always in style excepting the colors of political correctness.

Material thinkers, in their centers of power, created governments, laws, religions, and theories assumed them to be essential to civility. Power centers do not form spontaneously. They are the result of those who fear the loss of unearned wealth and power (egos) and consequently focus upon stopping apparent chaos. That is, without their civilization, we are led to believe man would brutalize himself. Yet, our survival throughout history and prehistory testifies to our persistence rather than our failure to cope. Actually it seems realistic all ideals, beliefs, and theories or isms have only been destructive in their consequences.

Here is a clear-minded statement of what guides actions: Civility is a function of the Principles of Existence, and we all have the capacity to exercise these principles at every moment. They guarantee the greatest possible gratification of our Value.

The struggle, constant vigilance, and sacrifices that are attributable to illusionary freedom and justice have never yielded civility. Whatever civility occurs happens only as the result of applied Value inside all of us.

These Principles of Existence form a morality that is truly self-serving by regulating our opportunism according to principles that satisfy everyone. These principles eliminate the need for governments, laws, and religions.

Well, I can understand just how befuddled this leaves those who are dependent upon material ways of thinking. Their first response would be outrageous anger at the insolence of this farmer telling them they haven't a clue what they are doing. They have all of history to verify their course, and what a sad course it is.

My question to material thinkers is, how are they going to change our course to something verifiably good when everything to date is the consequence of thinking materially? More of the freedom, justice, equality, and tolerance we have never achieved?

Imagine what would happen should justice or freedom prevail, especially together as we commonly assume. Freedom contradicts the application of justice and the demands of justice contradict freedom. Materialists have no choice but to name this futility, progress.

Part 7 - Really Genuine Progress

Some Thoughts about a Genuinely New World

I'm sure some people feel they must challenge the Value theory, but it is not a theory. Materialism is a theory because it is incomplete, requiring ideals, beliefs, commandments, laws, and conditional or specialized protocols to achieve what we are told is civilization. In this faked culture, corruption is endemic and pervasive. Civilized? Not at all.

Perceiving everything is made of Value answers all questions relevant to existence, including why, and doing so puts us in the driver's seat exercising the Principles of Existence all the time. All Value exists for self-gratification. The only creatures failing to understand this are humans, and it is because of thinking materially. Value perceiving is not an ism (theory).

We are in uncharted territory, with world culture functioning according to the material theory of existence while the correct Value Perspective is, for the most part, unknown.

The material theory of existence must be gutted and replaced with Value perceiving, and the sooner this happens the better. As we proceed down the material road, we are becoming ever more sophisticated at killing and creating an unhealthy and toxic environment. It is our Value inside us exhibiting intuitive measures of sanity and control. As egoistic leaders feel more and more threatened, they will sacrifice their own and our inner Value. Competition, the bluff, and pushing the red button is preferable to loss of face as the bluff is exposed.

Perhaps this has already happened in the Middle East, where the Media has overlooked the outrageous use of unconscionable or so-called "depleted" uranium munitions by our military. In their homeland, the residue of these munitions will remain seriously radioactive for thousands of years. It seems to me this must partly underlie the extreme, unalterable vengeance of fundamentalists and terrorists who could be absolutely justified in their condemnation of us if we have used depleted uranium munitions. (We never hear about this in the news!)

No other abuse I can think of would generate the level of extreme emotion we see when even women, their children, and now some US citizens participate in killing the evil they see. I cannot imagine a better example of the evil axiom of "Power makes right" in a materially envisioned reality.

If we accept the Value Perspective, here are some conditions we can derive about future governments, businesses, and other social organizations, as well as the way we personally think. In no particular order, they are as follows:

1. Institutions should never be given the legal status of a person. They are not a person and therefore have do not have the focus of a person but rather agendas other than the Principles of Existence based solely in money and power.

2. What genuine, nontransitory gratifications of existence we have been able to achieve are the result of our irrepressible intuited body of Value, not the rationales of material perception.

3. We must develop ways of living, especially for young families, that support life without incurring debt. Actually, pioneers of the wild have always had to do this.

4. We do not live to increase productivity. There is no harm in not having moneypower or toys.

5. We live to enjoy existence, not to fill a chart or graph presented by some material expert.

6. What we should be doing is creating an environment where every person is first inculcated with the Value Perspective and the Principles of Existence. It takes all of youth to do this!

7. With the Principles of Existence we can use the power formerly transferred to central authority to personally deal predictably and decisively with all the vagaries of existence.

8. From a material perspective, there are no keys to universal civility.

9. There are no free rides except in a materially visualized existence.

10. All ideals, rights, isms, and mythical salvations are faked.

11. Personally, I'll take chaos. Its unpredictable twists and turns build understanding and fluency—that is, character about existence that enable all of us to live by our own wits. It makes human relationships fluid, open, friendly, and enjoyable, as we are all on the same team.

12. We gain legitimacy. Being made of matter, we have no legitimate need to express anything. Only Value demands gratification universally as the legitimate or action-driven substance of all things. Material reasoning is a vacant yard in which we grow intellectual weeds. We can see this dilemma when expressions of Value reads so differently than material ways of thought. Materialism and all isms are nouns, concrete and inflexible. "Valuism" is not even a word, but if it were, it would be a verb, applicable to all motions of existence. This perspective changes everything!

13. The realistic solution to all humankind's problems resides in the application of the Principles of Existence emanating from the Value we are—that is, the body whole. This places the resolution of all problems directly in the lap of individuals, not governments, religions or other theories of existence.

14. The summed totality of materialism presented in this book rests largely upon the male leader. Generally, woman has supported and compensated for the whole of man's folly including reproduction and war. The human male has only one momentary function and then he absconds to impregnates the rest of the world with all the ridiculous ego building ideals, beliefs, theories, isms, and their ignorant protocols. The male calls this "progress" which is why progress is meaningfully indefinable. This faked progress exists to avoid the male ego's responsibilities to family, a responsibility women find more difficult to shirk.

15. Evolutionarily speaking, initiation of the Value Perspective is a dividing point in human intellectuality and evolution leading away from materialism and establishing genuine goodness for a legitimate and sustainable existence.

Education

    Education's first function must be to instill actively, passively, and continuously the Value Perspective in all people. It begins in the home with parents and adults who recognize the significance of the Value Perspective. From this perspective children will personally experience how the Principles of Existence are indeed the route to genuine gratification. For all of us, this happening makes continued existence even more worth possessing.

Jerry Hewes

Economics

In a materially perceived existence, no verifiable moral standard or goodness exists; neither standards proposed by the state nor religions prevail except artificially and ultimately destructively. All morality is superseded and overwritten by the underlying requirements of moneypower.

Underlying the deceiving ideals, corruption is the norm as money and unbridled opportunism are indelibly attached to material reasoning. For this reason, money and material reasoning represent all that is wrong with the human race.

Today, money is the means to the wholesale enslavement of mankind, generally not by brute force but through taxation, debt service, globalization, militarization, the stock market, bogus health care, legal entanglement, environmental control, mind control, illusion, and government—that is, material ways of thinking. Each of these are the deceptions we try to believe are good for our existence yet, these are the illusions we want to escape.

The legal framework of government has evolved to focus the flow of money away from us to ever greater concentrations of unearned money. This is the certainty we continuously fight as the legacy of those who deceive us. For us, playing this materialized game is equated with survival in a contrived competitive existence, and this vulnerability is moneypower in the driver's seat of our existence.

Consequently, we sense with certitude that something is wrong. We sense it because our minds and bodies are not material but rather made of Value and capable of sensing the caustic and demeaning environment of moneypower.

Materially speaking, money prevents all of us from reaching our potential by diverting our thoughts to the presumed benefits of lying, cheating, back stabbing, fraud, taxation, profiteering, skimming, perversion, and all the other forms of usury and predation available to materially thinking minds, including the printing and maintenance of a currency whose Value is the playground for speculation, opportunism, and deceit.

Some complain of the evils of an arbitrary or fiat currency, but there exists no currency that is not a fiat currency. Gold fails the test miserably, gyrating wildly against currencies, but not because it has intrinsic Value. Gold has very little intrinsic Value. A bushel of oats is immeasurably higher in intrinsic Value than a gold bar. Gold is Valued because it represents the illusion of permanence and therefore is hoarded and materially central in our thoughts.

One of the few moments when gold loses its fiat rating and moves from something to look at, to real Value, is when a gold bar hits you aside the head. It's real stuff but then to, so is a rock. Then there is the symbolism of commitment so deeply felt as to be eternal. Gold is the standard but nothing is eternal because it must be sold to those equally deceived to realize its Value.

Every currency is fiat. That is not the problem. The problem is finding a standard for the Value of money. It must be undeniable and stable, yet it must accommodate changes dictated by the users. There is no such currency to be chosen by material thinkers because money is their means to profit unconscionably by deception, manipulation, and speculation, generating unearned money instead of meaningful (undeniable and stable) collateral.

Amoral money is collected by speculation, stock market, stock market racketeering, debt service, loan sharking, protection, skimming, profiteering, financial services, taxation, and gifting. The identifying character of such money is unearned wealth accumulated by some form of scheming.

Despite the rhetoric, there is no intellectually valid morality attached to the giving of unearned wealth (philanthropy) detached from those who produced it. Those who hold large quantities of what must be unearned money can manipulate almost anyone to their purpose, but the intrinsic morality of wealth belongs to the producers of wealth, not those having wealth far beyond personal needs that has been skimmed from the producers or by speculations.

If there is any truth to the validity of governments, we must identify what it is and keep all the mechanisms 100% open and simple enough for public understanding and regulation. There is one currency that stands this test, and it is the hour. Everyone knows what it is and can judge its relationship with Values quickly. Generally, it becomes very obvious when an hour's meaning has been cheated.

When all people use the same financial standard, rationality creates a lock-step agreement that changes only when all concerned people agree to a change. In other words, speculation becomes illogical as well as immoral not only because we all agree as to Value's substance but also because unearned wealth is seen as immoral from the Value Perspective.

Perhaps one of the hardest things to criticize is the concept of compassion. Material plenty coupled with unearned wealth (taxation, profiteering, and debt service) has made possible huge funding of what we like to think is compassionate goodness, typically in the form of foundations and government funding. Despite its alleged morality, this form of giving has always been disconnected from genuine moral conduct because we cannot agree upon the definition of "moral," and because morality is not conferred with money. Indeed, every individual must in some manner earn his own way. This is compassion in action.

The idea should not be to end compassion but rather to end unearned wealth that supports a faked or hyped morality. The Principles of Existence enforce the concept of no free rides and make compassion your decision.

We need to realize that economics cannot be genuinely reformed without the reform of morality and the Value Perspective defines truly life-enhancing moral guides to existence. Character does matter.

As we learn more, some of us drop this egoized effort to rape or save the world, but this is because our minds finally realize that something is wrong. It is that material thinking is bogus and we need to be gratified in ways that are not addressed by material ways of thinking.

This realization leaves definition in our hands as we apply the now intellectualized Principles of Existence essential to all legitimate things of existence.

Two takeaways are not immediately evident from this discourse but are concrete maxims that originate from an understanding of the implications of these principles.

There are no free rides in existence. Everyone must in some way earn his own existence. In an existence where everything is made of Value, it is clear that morality or the Principles of Existence makes the decisions defining what is good.

Unearned wealth is immoral. With unearned wealth comes the apparent freedom to escape the consequences of your ignorance and for this reason we must establish a stable currency, because unearned wealth is only clearly definable with a stable and universal currency, the hour.

Self-Acceptance

Self-acceptance may seem like an odd Principle of Existence because it directly affects no one but ourselves. It is an internal happening, automatically growing bit by bit as contradictions are eliminated. Its effect upon your Value is contentment.

With self-acceptance comes a confidence enabling infecting others with thoughts capable of liberating their minds to see the benefits of the Value Perspective.

Self-acceptance is materially impossible as material ideals (illusions) are indefinite and unreachable automatically making one a failure. Then too, material contradictions or anger issues destroy integrity and drive one to achieve goals that involve the compromise of self to the growth of ego.

Despite the rhetoric of ego, the subpar performance of ego on the scale of self-acceptance is the underlying cause of man's need to rape the world all because he views existence materially.

This leaves any apparently well intentioned material mind with ego-driven do-good-ism. It is done to achieve a substitute body of self-acceptance and the apparent contentment and confidence it offers as ego gratification by illusion.

We must recognize the Value we are, and it has nothing to do with do-good-ism/philanthropy that is intended to change sociology and economics without that change arising as a function of the recipients own understanding and consequential actions of the recipients own Value. In-other-words, teach and provide an environment leading to understanding of existence and let people do as they will. This is the consequence of self-acceptance.

Conspiracy

Like opportunism, *cooperation* is natural to the human mind. It is our way of expressing agreement and respect. There is no reason to think conspiracy is a bad thing except when existence is perceived as a material (occult or secret and behind closed doors) happening that needs ideals, rights, gods, and other imaginary controls, in that always failing effort to regulate human conduct.

Under the material vision of existence, neither opportunism nor conspiracy has a bona fide morality. Both are exploited under the banners of laws and commandments, which are human creations that have no rationality on which to base their thinking except ideals, beliefs, and gods.

The trick of material (and consequently bad) conspiracies is to make us think everything is natural when it is actually a secret manipulation of our existence. It is done for the material purposes of raising unearned money and increasing control and the usual conspiracy, scamming, monopolistic control, intimidation, deceiving opportunism, debt service, or formation of governments, taxation and killings of those who threaten exposure.

The Value Perspective stops the bad aspects of conspiracy dead in its tracks. Apply the Principles of Existence and all relationships are guided by noncontradiction and honesty, respect, thoughtfulness, cooperation, and self-acceptance. There is no reason to have closed doors. Under the banner of the Value Perspective, conspiracies are the consequence of thoughtfulness and cooperation that benefits everybody.

The first and genuine task of education is to conspire to instill the Value Perspective and the consequential Principles of Existence in the minds of every young person. The Value Perspective is such a magnificent release from the bondage of a materially perceived existence underlying our thought. It is to create a new human existence beyond the scope of anything thought possible. Genuine intellectual understanding of existence that does not involve all the flimflams of illusions and deceiving methodologies required to make faked civilization almost palatable.

Materially, the evil of conspiracy is always present with accumulation of directionless unearned money because of the absence of bona fide morality.

For this reason, taxation and debt must be eliminated from the human psyche and labeled contradictory. We have accepted them as necessary evils but they are not moral in any sense because both of them sell a future that is not determined by us but by governments and lenders.

- A "necessary evil" is just a way of slipping contradictions into unsuspecting minds. It is one of the more easily identified lies used to support deceptions that cannot or will not explain why materially necessitated contradictions appear so essential.

- Genuine goodness—that is, existence with understanding—is a function of the contents of people's minds and only becomes definable and apparent when the Principles of Existence are evidenced through demeanor, conversation, and actions in the realm of chaos or absence of state control.

That taxation and debt are an accepted part of culture has plagued Western culture for thousands of years. In the past and today whatever inconsequential control we may have had of our governments is now lost completely to the influence of unearned money. For this reason the lead in most meaningful investigations is "follow the money," certifying that there is little morality in the function of many organizations, including our government.

Representation has always been a myth. But now, through lack of effective leadership, this myth has led us to worldwide corruption in the name of globalism and the malignant Old Methodologies but New Scale World Order (OMNSWO). Yes, we need globalism, but not what we are being sold through hidden conspiracies beyond our awareness that culturally manipulate and tax us to achieve a control by methodologies no different than in the past.

The only globalism we need is a universal understanding that brings all minds together for the common purpose of Value gratification as defined by the Principles of Existence. As the Principles of Existence replace governmental control, all of what is supported by taxes becomes unnecessary. That which is necessary will easily be supported voluntarily if it is perceived as genuinely good.

Say and think what you may. I am saying things that must be said if we are to prevail on earth. For those who wish to escape materialism by alien technology, I say good-bye. Einstein wishes you well, for Einstein says, in effect, that you are delusional. In Einstein's material existence alien salvation is impossible.

Debt manipulation is a big way in which the world is run today. Nobody in Washington or our state capitals will approve of eliminating debt. Eliminating debt is completely consistent with the Principles of Existence, but it means we must reorganize the way we think and the way we live so that borrowing becomes unnecessary. It is our world. Let's do it! Let's take charge.

We must become a pay-as-you-go culture. Debt is a scamming trick of the money changers (today's banks) where money changers loan money they do not have but that you must repay in full with genuine cash. All a bank has to accomplish is the appearance of solvency which is backed by taxpayers today. But you repay the full amount plus interest. This repayment is many times larger than the bank cash used to cover your loan due to "fractional reserve" banking. This practice generates a huge level of profitability and is the amoral foundation of much unearned money.

A new world is impossible if we continue to think materially with all the illusions about independence, freedom, justice, rights, wealth and how these illusions fail to fulfill us. Despite our expectations in a materially conceived existence, the recipients of taxes and debt service fees to accumulate unearned money, have no ability to define goodness except with illusions. They find their existence tied to keeping us deceived about how life cannot be successfully lived without them. They name their demise chaos or anarchy. Fear is their mechanism of control.

From the Value Perspective, anarchy is reality. The Principles of Existence exist inside all of us. Chaos is used in physics to describe systems that we can define in great detail but whose internal actions we cannot predict, even if we can determine the overall or external effect of the system. Chaos is not something to fear but rather is natural to dynamic or Value directed systems, such as flow of water and human culture under the influence of a correct perspective. Chaos is the vital and stimulating part of existence whose outcome can be predicted, not in any specific event but rather in individual fulfillment, when the Principles of Existence are applied, as the actions essential to existence.

Here is a quote from Margaret Rouse about chaos theory (March 2009, http://www.whatis.techtarget.com/definition/chaos-theory):

"Although chaos is often thought to refer to randomness and lack of order, it is more accurate to think of it as an apparent randomness that results from complex systems and interactions among systems. According to James Gleick, author of *Chaos: Making a New Science*, chaos theory is "a revolution not of technology, like the laser revolution or the computer revolution, but a revolution of ideas. This revolution began with a set of ideas having to do with disorder in nature: from turbulence in fluids to the erratic flows of epidemics … It has continued with an even broader set of ideas that might be better classified under the rubric of complexity."

Obviously, this complexity serves the need of our minds to remain active in determining our course. Chaos (anarchy) is not an enemy of civil conduct; it is a friend, a dear friend bringing inner civility to light. We should hold chaos close to our heart because it opens the door to our individual authority to practice the culture we desire.

Freedom

We run wild with our heads held high, our arms thrown back, our hair flowing in the breeze, only to discover we must still feed, clothe, house ourselves, and deal with all the vagaries of existence. If we are far enough away from the civilization that promises freedom or justice and their unstated servitude and sacrifices, we may escape the perverted demands of unearned wealth (taxation) and the justice we have yet to name revenge. It is the justice concerned with hiding its own ignorance under a robe rather than teaching how to avoid building a culture profligate with injustice.

Freedom means having no restrictions or qualifications. The freedom we carelessly assume is really unrelated to existence, human or otherwise. Nothing is free except perhaps our minds' ability to imagine anything.

Freedom is not something to be sought by constant vigilance and sacrifice unless one thinks materially. Freedom is an illusion, and for this reason freedom is popular among egos that need causes and the intellectual space to enact them (materiality). Because freedom is so appealing, charlatans of illusion called politicians, bait the human intellect that is discontented with what materialism (chasing freedom) has created. The only substance of freedom is the lack of coercion and restraint, which means we are free to kill, cheat, steal, and so on.

"Well, we didn't mean it that way." Is there another way to define it? This freedom is nothing but a deceptive tactic of immoral opportunists, the ones who know nothing of the Principles of Existence. Why not apply the vigilance freedom requires to vigilance about the Principles of Existence? These principles offer a highly improved quality of existence and can be taught daily by example in the home.

Morality

Because we have assumed a material existence, we find ourselves without moral guidance and must create it. Well, there we have it. On the street corner nearest you is a moralist selling any morality you want. Oh, to be sure he sells only the highest quality, for there is no higher standard, just any standard you want.

There is no basis for any of it, and something inside tells us we have no understanding of the problem. Well, let's go for understanding then. Well ... er ... uh ... no comprehensive understanding of existence is possible from a materially envisioned existence. The absence of meaningful reason and the resultant inclusions of contradictory ways of thinking prevents understanding.

Universality? No problem. This morality decrees that disagreement cannot be. Supply the power to enforce your morality, and universality is ours.

We have named this realm of sought for control civilation. The reason modern morality has failed us is that it has no foundation. It is rationally unsupportable. Current morality is completely imaginary because it originates out of material thinking that has by its nature excluded rationality. Material things have no reason to do anything and must receive their morality from gods and governments.

We possess a mind. To be sure some would say a God-given mind, but they say this simply because the source of material morality has no foundation and must look to gods. Whatever is decreed as moral must have a superpower foundation. And yes, our minds desire understanding enough to demand it even if it has to be imaginary.

Understanding has mistakenly been sought via knowledge, but a collection of facts has to be integrated to reach understanding. Integration demands something heretofore unconsidered by the intellectual elite excepting the scorned Ayn Rand. No mind can integrate anything containing contradictions. Consequently, any mind accustomed to material ways of thinking cannot integrate facts, because a material reality is loaded with contradictions that are natural to illusionary thinking. This verifies that, as material assumers, we consider an understanding of existence to be impossible.

If one expects to exist, noncontradiction is king, as Ayn Rand observed. Being intellectually noncontradictory depends upon the application of the principles included within the principle of noncontradiction.

These principles say everything there is to say about morality. Everything else, including everything governments are supposed to control and indoctrinate, is simply the unsuccessful attempt to fake civility. This includes the four great axioms of materialism: "Knowledge is power," "Power makes right," "In God we trust," and salvation. That is, escapism, the material world of today and forever. Material thinking offers nothing more for our minds.

Our democracy is the greatest myth ever to sully man's mind. To think that another person could represent you in any manner excepting the application of the six Principles of Existence, is barn-floor scrapings. No, it is far worse. It is mind-obliterating self-destructiveness.

Trust

Trust only arises when man operates according to principles, because principles are universal and incorporated in all minds. Application of these principles has as its consequence the greatest gratifications possible for anything of existence, including man.

Four axioms arise from the material perceptions of existence. They are "Knowledge is power," "Power makes right," "In God we trust," and "salvation." Despite all the attempts to make our culture just and free—socialism, democracy, communism, materialism, capitalism, totalitarianism, heaven, salvation, nirvana, and so on—all of it is nothing but hype. To believe noodle-minded egos with their faked approaches to existence is to condemn us to noodle-minded madness or insanity. These approaches are all loaded with contradictions and can only masquerade as civilization.

It cannot be stressed strongly enough how everything today is simply garbage, the fillers of ignorance, silence, tolerance, inaction, and unbridled opportunism or... the products of a materially visualized existence.

Cooperation's function is to generate happiness and security. It does this through the symbiosis of minds who understand one another because each knows what is in the other's mind. This kind of trust and the happiness it brings are only available through the Value Perspective and its Principles of Existence.

Government

In a world full of assumptions and resulting contradictions, governments do very little that is legitimate. Government's singular legitimate function can only be to ensure the Principles of Existence are the rule of the land. How much government can legitimately do beyond this is a function of ***cooperation*** and the openness to insure that it is cooperation, not "representation."

Should the Value Perspective become universal, what is our future? It is not my decision to make except as a participating individual and opportunist guided by the Principles of Existence. But this is for sure, all governmental actions would require consensus or total harmony, not a majority vote. Government would have to argue every complaint and always rule by the Principles of Existence.

Around the globe and throughout our culture, we are experiencing material opportunism with no understanding of the proper way out. This reality has always been moneypower reaching for total control. First it was identified as Money Changers, then Robber Barons. Now we have named them Illuminati, Bilderberg, the New World Order, the Network, and Globalists or the Old Methodologies New Scale World Order with which current politicians have coevolved to be OMNSWO's marionettes.

Speaking materially and evolutionarily, democracy of today is nothing more than an illusion, a faked and fraudulent sign twirling by one chain in the dust and wind on the road of Power Makes Right.

Should we move to the Value Perspective, all of us will determine the parameters of culture and life becomes our pleasure to participate in a worldwide culture of gratifying our Value according to the Principles of Existence.

Conclusion

From the Value Perspective, we can now see the termination of human presence on earth if we persist in thinking materially. The best we can hope for is remote pockets of humanity escaping the insanity of material thinking. Whether these groups think materially or from the Value Perspective will determine man's future.

Intelligence or awareness is a ubiquitous quality developed not by genes but by the ability to perceive correctly. Evolutionarily speaking, we have had our chance to prove the success of intelligence in movies exemplifying failed intellectuality like The Matrix and Star Wars. But intelligence is a misunderstood word that fails to grasp that all animals and things are intelligent given their environment and physical realities. Actually, our existence is founded in the predictability of everything or the awareness of all things to do as the principle of noncontradiction requires.

Today, all things deal with reality better than we do. We are the ones who fake reality and egoistically try to claim intelligence for ourselves alone for the purpose of sustaining favored status in God's imaginary universe. In-other-words claimed intelligence is the consequential need to eliminate the insignificance and ignorance of self in a materially visualized existence.

With the advent of language, we have developed the capacity to extensively deceive both ourselves and other people. When understanding is impossible, deception is inevitable. Here lies the origins of ego. The real issue is whether we will become aware of this problem and all its perversions of human life.

Awareness of the adverse effects of ego is typically sensed but never genuinely grasped until one changes to the Value Perspective and begins the intellectual process of exposing deception and discovering truth, leading to an understanding of existence.

This understanding is acquired slowly, but each step is rewarding. Each step confirms the Value of your own mind by recognition of its success in a realm where understanding was previously impossible. Each new awareness gives you more control, not only your own life but also, in a very real and personal sense, the evolution of all existence.

What I say is offered in an effort to genuinely help the evolution of goodness as seen from the Value Perspective, my perspective. This book is an exposé whose details you must personally verify. Successful life is your ability to share and to convince others of the rational thought that will determine our future, not the counting of toys.

Think of your life as an experience in learning to define goodness rather than trying to avoid the consequences of material thought with guaranteed ignorance. They are not important, no matter how important they seem. Remember Mark Twain's quote— "Never argue with stupid [unaware] people; they will drag you down to their level and then beat you with experience."

You can make the choices that overwhelmingly gratify you with genuine self-appreciation and acceptance if you follow the Principles of Existence, especially thoughtfulness, cooperation, and the confidence and contentment of self-acceptance. They put you in charge at the top. Something confident, open, harmonious silence bestows to character as a function of understanding.

Wow

If character was a function of beliefs, what principles would define existence? If character was a function of freedom, what principles would define character? If character was a function of justice, what principles would define character? What principles would knowledge evoke to define character? What principles would we employ for beliefs, freedom, justice, and knowledge to create harmony, or personal contentment, and peace? And where would our emotions be in all the resulting conflicts? What if character was a function of understanding of existence?

Would not character have the same grounding in all people? Would not we all have character of true integrity, that knows and employs the Principles of Existence? Has anyone ever considered a nation full of people who express character in chorus actually defining the quality of a culture, nation, and existence?

<u>Starry Night Publishing</u>

Everyone has a story...

Don't spend your life trying to get published! Don't tolerate rejection! Don't do all the work and allow the publishing companies reap the rewards!

Millions of independent authors like you, are making money, publishing their stories now. Our technological know-how will take the headaches out of getting published. Let "Starry Night Publishing.Com" take care of the hard parts, so you can focus on writing. You simply send us your Word Document and we do the rest. It really is that simple!

The big companies want to publish only "celebrity authors," not the average book-writer. It's almost impossible for first-time authors to get published today. This has led many authors to go the self-publishing route. Until recently, this was considered "vanity-publishing." You spent large sums of your money, to get twenty copies of your book, to give to relatives at Christmas, just so you could see your name on the cover. Now, however, the self-publishing industry allows authors to get published in a timely fashion, retain the rights to your work, keeping up to ninety-percent of your royalties, instead of the traditional five-percent.

We've opened up the gates, allowing you inside the world of publishing. While others charge you as much as fifteen-thousand dollars for a publishing package, we charge less than five-hundred dollars to cover copyright, ISBN, and distribution costs. Do you really want to spend all your time formatting, converting, designing a cover, and then promoting your book, because no one else will?

Our editors are professionals, able to create a top-notch book that you will be proud of. Becoming a published author is supposed to be fun, not a hassle.

At Starry Night Publishing, you submit your work, we create a professional-looking cover, a table of contents, compile your text and images into the appropriate format, convert your files for eReaders, take care of copyright information, assign an ISBN, allow you to keep one-hundred-percent of your rights, distribute your story worldwide on Amazon, Barnes & Noble and many other retailers, and write you a check for your royalties. There are no other hidden fees involved! You don't pay extra for a cover, or to keep your book in print. We promise! Everything is included! You even get a free copy of your book and unlimited half-price copies.

In four short years, we've published more than fifteen-hundred books, compared to the major publishing houses which only add an average of six new titles per year. We will publish your fiction, or non-fiction books about anything, and look forward to reading your stories and sharing them with the world.

We sincerely hope that you will join the growing Starry Night Publishing family, become a published author and gain the world-wide exposure that you deserve. You deserve to succeed. Success comes to those who make opportunities happen, not those who wait for opportunities to happen. You just have to try. Thanks for joining us on our journey.

www.starrynightpublishing.com

www.facebook.com/starrynightpublishing/

Made in the USA
Las Vegas, NV
14 May 2021

23053562R00095